BEYOND
QUESTION PERIOD

or What really goes on in Ottawa

ROY CULLEN

Order this book online at www.trafford.com
or email orders@trafford.com

Most Trafford titles are also available at major online book retailers.

Printed in the United States of America.

ISBN: 978-1-4269-6946-1 (sc)
ISBN: 978-1-4269-6947-8 (hc)
ISBN: 978-1-4269-6948-5 (e)

Library of Congress Control Number: 2011907885

Trafford rev. 05/17/2011

 www.trafford.com

North America & international
toll-free: 1 888 232 4444 (USA & Canada)
phone: 250 383 6864 ✦ fax: 812 355 4082

Dedicated to the people of Etobicoke North, Toronto,
for the honour and privilege of representing them, and all Canadians,
in the House of Commons in Ottawa from 1996 to 2008.

BEYOND QUESTION PERIOD
or What really goes on in Ottawa

Contents

Preface

Surveys have shown that over ninety per cent of Canadians trust firefighters. High on the list also are nurses, pharmacists, airline pilots, doctors and police officers. At the very bottom of the list are national politicians and car salespeople with only seven per cent of Canadians indicating that they find these people to be trustworthy. This is indeed a sad commentary on our political system (and on car dealerships!). Too often politicians become a popular scapegoat or 'whipping boy' for citizens who are venting their frustrations about the economy or the world in general, or as a means of expressing themselves about challenges in their own personal life. Having said that, elected officials can often be the authors of their own misfortune when they break promises, exhibit childlike behavior, and engage in unprofessional or illegal activities.

Over the years it has struck me that Canadians do not have a very complete view of what goes on in Ottawa, and what their members of parliament do. I was often asked questions about how I split my time between Ottawa, Toronto, and other work related travel; about what sort of accommodation I had in Ottawa; about how I traveled back and forth between Toronto and Ottawa; about what budgetary resources were available to me to function as an MP; about fundraising methods and strategies; and generally about what is was like to be an MP.

Time and time again citizens who come to Ottawa and spend a few hours or days on parliament hill leave the nation's capital with a much less jaundiced view of how their country is governed. Citizens often see Ottawa through the prism of Question Period which is but a microcosm—and a theatrical one at that—of events and activities on the Hill.

By and large, the federal MPs in Ottawa that I have had the honour and pleasure to work with, when I served as an MP for twelve and one half years, are talented people who are motivated to make Canada a better place in which to live—and they work very hard to make this happen. Naturally, like in any occupation or profession, there are some 'bad apples', but in my experience they are very much the exception to the general rule.

Since not every Canadian will have the opportunity to see what goes on in Ottawa first hand, this book is an attempt to paint a picture for them in the hope that they will have a better understanding of the work and life of an MP, together with an understanding of how decisions are made in their nation's capital. The personal examples and stories provided herein are inserted to bring the subject matter to life and are not meant to be autobiographical in nature. While I am very proud of the work I accomplished serving the country I love as an MP, I have no delusions about my contribution which, in the overall scheme of things—was a modest one. While I have always been a team player—an attribute which has flowed from my active participation in team sports in school, university and other venues—I would say that during my stint in Ottawa, even though I took on some senior roles, I was generally not part of the *party establishment* and I operated somewhat independently. This perhaps allows me to view life in Ottawa on the hill more objectively, with the goal in mind of educating Canadians about a very important institution – our parliament.

As author Malcolm Gladwell has noted, "Curiosity about the interior life of other people's day—to—day work is one of the most fundamental of human impulses….."[1]

In the next pages, I will attempt to describe how the Parliament of Canada works; how MPs are engaged in the decision—making process; and how it 'feels' to be an MP. The political process, including the nomination process and election campaigns, will also be described. The work and responsibilities of an MP both on parliament hill and in the constituency will be covered. Personal anecdotes will be used, not to aggrandize individual contributions or impact, but rather to try to bring to life some of the challenges and opportunities of an MP.

After reading this I hope you have a better appreciation of what a member of parliament does and about how the machinery of government in Ottawa works. If you do, I will have accomplished my objective.

---

1   Malcolm Gladwell, *What the Dog Saw*, (New York: Little , Brown and Company, 2009)

Canada's Parliament – A Proud Institution

Canadians seem to me to have a love/hate relationship with their federal parliament in Ottawa. On the one hand many Canadians, me included, believe that our parliament often exudes child—like behavior and is often not focused on matters that are really important to our citizens. The growth of tabloid journalism has contributed to an excessive coverage of the sensational, and regrettably to the baser instincts of citizens. On the other hand, Canadians follow events in Ottawa carefully and they see what goes on there as important and impactful on their lives. Regrettably a certain cynicism has developed about the integrity and capabilities of MPs and Senators. This cynicism has fostered apathy and voter turnout has diminished over the years. In the general election held on October 14, 2008, for example, only 58.8% of eligible Canadians cast a ballot. This is a problem that needs to be addressed. I believe that the advent of regional parties, like the Bloc Québécois and the Reform Party, have made the House of Commons a more partisan place and heightened immature behavior. Although there are no 'magic bullets', we should look at the following as ways of reducing voter apathy and cynicism –

- the Speaker and MPs should take steps to improve the decorum of members during Question Period;
- politicians should be much less callous about promising things they can't deliver; and,
- MPs and Senators need to be more mindful of the fact that they are subjected to, and rightly so, a very high standard of honesty and ethical behavior – and they should act accordingly.

The Parliament of Canada is modeled after Britain's Parliament - referred to as the Westminster model. Unlike presidential forms of government like those in the U.S.A. and Russia, our country's leader, the prime minister, is the leader of the political party that wins the most seats in the House of Commons following a general election, and is able to form a government.

In our form of government, it is very useful, if you are the governing party, to have the prime minister and all of the cabinet ministers in your own caucus. Access to them is very readily available—unlike a presidential type of government where the president and the cabinet ministers are not in parliament. I would often discuss issues important to me and my constituents with ministers and sometimes the prime minister when in caucus on Wednesday mornings or in the chamber of the House of Commons. Meetings with them were relatively easy to organize as well.

At the time of publishing, the 41st Parliament was coming into being following the May 2, 2011 general election, but some seats were still being contested.

In Canada's 40th Parliament—the one that came about as a result of the October 14th, 2008 general election—the Conservative Party of Canada had formed a minority government.

The Conservative Party of Canada (CPC) was able to govern, with the confidence of the House of Commons, with 145 of the 308 seats (or 47% of the total). The Liberal Party, together with the NDP and the Bloc Québécois, had the capacity to vote against the Conservative Party (as they threatened to do with the aborted coalition agreement that was signed in December 2008, and finally did so on a non-confidence motion on March 25, 2011) on a matter of confidence, the minority government would be defeated and Canada's Governor General would either dissolve Parliament and call a general election, or ask another Party or group within Parliament to form a government. The May 2, 2011 was the result of the March 25, 2011 Liberal non-confidence motion that was supported by the majority of MPs in the House of Commons.

Province / Territory	C.P.C.	Lib.	B.Q.	N.D.P.	Ind.	Vacant	Total
PARTY STANDINGS 40th Parliament							
Alberta	27			1			28
British Columbia	22	5		9			36
Manitoba	9	1		4			14
New Brunswick	6	3		1			10
Newfoundland and Labrador		6		1			7
Nova Scotia	4	5		2			11
Nunavut	1						1
Ontario	51	38		17			106
Prince Edward Island	1	3					4
Quebec	11	14	48	1	1		75
Saskatchewan	13	1					14
Northwest Territories				1			1
Yukon		1					1
TOTAL	145	77	48	37	1		308

(Source: Parliament of Canada web site)

Representation in the House of Commons is based largely on the concept of 'representation by population' or 'rep—by—pop'. Given Canada's current population of 33½ million people, and with 308 seats in the House of Commons, this translates into an average of 108,766 people per constituency. This figure of 108,766 is very close to the population of Etobicoke North because it is a fairly typical urban riding. In Canada, however, representation—by—population falls away for the Province of Prince Edward Island. Under strict representation—by—population, P.E.I (122,000 population) would be entitled to only one seat. But it's guaranteed four. New Brunswick (population 750,000) should really only have seven seats but it is guaranteed ten.

Canada works on the 'first past the post' and not a proportional electoral system. While I appreciate and respect those Canadians who would like us to adopt a system of proportional representation in Canada, I remain firmly committed to a 'first past the post' electoral system.

The most compelling argument for proportional representation can be interpreted from the two tables which follow. On the basis of these results the Green Party, under a proportional representation system following the 2008 general election in Canada, would have been awarded 21 seats (6.8% of the 308 seats in the House of Commons) based on their attaining

3

6.8% of the popular. Instead, because the Green Party candidates were not 'first past the post' in any of the election campaigns across Canada, the result was not one seat in the House of Commons. In the 2011 election, the popular vote for the Green Party was diminished, but their leader, Elizabeth May, secured a seat in the House of Commons.

At the time of publishing this book, the May 2, 2011 general election had just been completed with many surprising and unprecedented results. The Stephen Harper Conservative Party will form a majority government for the first time; the Bloc Québec was virtually eliminated in the Province of Québec; the New Democratic Party will head into unchartered waters as the Official Opposition in the House of Commons; and the Green Party successfully elected their leader Elizabeth May to the House of Commons - another first.

2011 Canadian Election Results

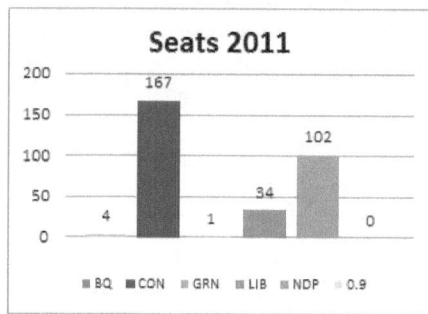 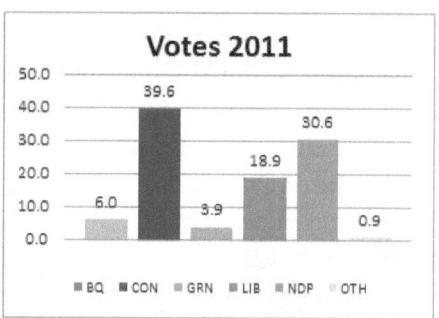

Source: Andrew Heard, Political Science Department — Simon Fraser University

IMPORTANT UPDATE: The normal validation of polling station totals in a Quebec riding resulted in a new winner being declared after the election. François Lapointe (NDP) - Montmagny--L'Islet--Kamouraska--Rivière-du-Loup, QC - won by 5 votes (0.01% margin) after the validated count reversed the election night win of 100 votes by his opponent Bernard Généreux (CON). A judicial recount is underway. If confirmed then the seat totals for the 2011 election on this page will change. Two other recounts are pending.

2008 Canadian Election Results

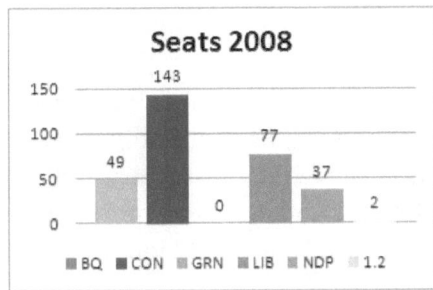
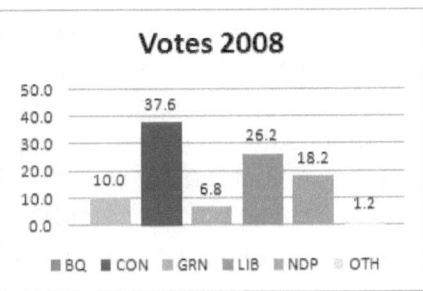

Source: Andrew Heard, Political Science Department — Simon Fraser University

In my view, however, the disadvantages of proportional representation far outweigh the plusses. In my view the three negatives are the following –

- encourages splinter parties and perpetual minority governments;
- lack of direct accountability between local voters and elected representatives (I will expand on this below); and,
- faulty and undemocratic process for the selection of party candidates.

Meeting with elected Members of the Assembly of the Republic in Portugal in April 2007 in advance of Portugal's term as President of the European Union convinced me that proportional representation lacked the accountability that Canadians demanded.

These representatives had been placed on lists by their respective parties, in priority order, and won a seat in the Portuguese Assembly based on whether or not they were above or below the cut off line based on the percentage of the vote their political party had won–not very democratic in my judgment considering the lack of regional run—offs.

I recall asking these representatives how a Portuguese citizen living in Lisbon would seek help from a Member of the Assembly on a matter relating to a national healthcare issue. Because there are no locally elected representatives, I was told that a citizen with such a query, unless they knew, or knew of, a particular representative, would probably place a call to the switchboard at the National Assembly and they would be referred to a member of the Standing Committee on Health.

Contrast this approach to what would happen in Canada if an individual was seeking answers to a federal healthcare issue. This person would communicate with his/her local MP and if they considered that the response from the MP was not satisfactory, they would vote for another candidate at the next election if all else failed. This, to me, is accountability and this direct link to one's elected official incents them to listen and act on the concerns of the citizenry.

Being ushered into the House of Commons to take one's seat for the first time is quite an amazing experience. According to tradition, new members are supposed to appear to be dragged to their place, but I offered little resistance to Prime Minister Chrétien and Minister of National Defense David Collenette when they introduced me to the House and the Speaker and I was shown my seat!

David Collenette and Prime Minister Chrétien ushering me into the House of Commons for the first time in 1996

In the 1993 general election, my party won 177 seats (out of a total of 295). With 60 % of the seats, this was clearly a majority government for the Liberal Party. In fact, whereas normally the government members sit to the right of the speaker (designated # 5 in figure below) I, and about 30 of my Liberal colleagues sat in what is affectionately called 'the rump' on the same side as the opposition members (designated #6 in figure below) and next to the speaker. The rump actually gives you a good vantage point for viewing the government ministers on the opposite side of the chamber and you get to vote last on the government side which can also be a plus since you are able to see first how all of your colleagues are voting.

The House of Commons Chamber

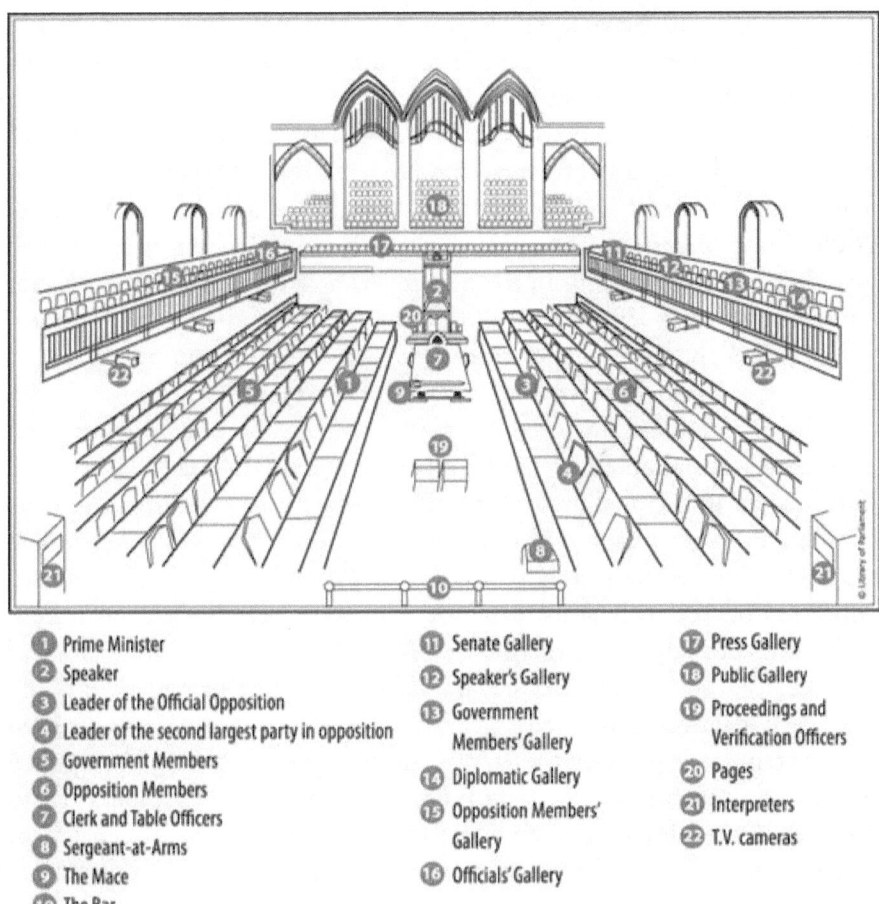

① Prime Minister	⑪ Senate Gallery	⑰ Press Gallery
② Speaker	⑫ Speaker's Gallery	⑱ Public Gallery
③ Leader of the Official Opposition	⑬ Government	⑲ Proceedings and
④ Leader of the second largest party in opposition	Members' Gallery	Verification Officers
⑤ Government Members	⑭ Diplomatic Gallery	⑳ Pages
⑥ Opposition Members	⑮ Opposition Members'	㉑ Interpreters
⑦ Clerk and Table Officers	Gallery	㉒ T.V. cameras
⑧ Sergeant-at-Arms	⑯ Officials' Gallery	
⑨ The Mace		
⑩ The Bar		

Source: HOUSE OF COMMONS PROCEDURE AND PRACTICE SECOND EDITION, 2009

Canada has a bicameral parliament meaning that we have two legislative chambers. Approximately half of the world's sovereign states are presently unicameral, including countries like the People's Republic of China, Cuba, Cyprus and New Zealand.

We have a lower house of parliament, being the House of Commons, an upper house, being the Senate, and of course the monarchy represented by the Governor General.

Currently, the Senate, which provides "regional" representation, has 105 members appointed by the Governor General on the advice of the prime minister, to serve until age 75.

Members are elected to the House of Commons whereas senators are appointed. Much controversy has centered on the partisan nature of Senate appointments and the fact that they are not elected. In December 2008, Prime Minister Stephen Harper appointed eighteen new senators to give their party a majority in the Senate. As a result of a series of Liberal governments from 1993 until 2006, the Senate had become 'stacked' with Liberal appointees, and from time—to—time the upper chamber, according to some, has thwarted the will of the House of Commons.

The Senate is meant to be the place for 'sober second thought', and as a means of enhancing regional representation. The Senate is divided into four main regional areas: Ontario, Quebec, the Maritimes, and the Western Provinces, each with 24 seats. The Territories also enjoy Senate representation as does Newfoundland & Labrador; the latter with an allocation of six Senate seats, while the Northwest Territories, the Yukon, and Nunavut each hold one seat.

Because they are not elected, nor do they have to worry about being reelected, senators can often offer an objective view on issues, free to some extent from partisan bias and focused on what is good public policy for Canada. Of course it is never quite this simple because Liberal Party senators, for example, are quite sensitive to the political dimension of issues – and if they forget, their colleagues in the House of Commons are sure to remind them!

I have found senators to be generally very capable and hardworking individuals who are committed in the extreme to providing good government to Canadians. They can on occasion improve bills that have originated in the House of Commons. Some of the toughest questions I ever had when presenting government bills, and my own private members' bill on user fees, to parliamentary committees came from the members of the Senate standing committees.

While I have followed the debate on Senate reform with interest, to me it is somewhat of an academic question when considering whether or not to make the Senate an elected body. Given our constitutional hurdles, and the vested interest of the major provinces, in my view it is unlikely that fundamental change will come soon, if ever. In any case, I am not convinced that we need another elected house. Notwithstanding the criticisms, it is my view that the Senate, while not perfect, performs a useful and vital role for Canadians the way it is currently constituted.

***

How does one get elected, and serve, in the House of Commons? The first and most important step is to be nominated by a political party to be that party's candidate in the next federal election. It is possible to run as an independent, but the chances of electoral success are slim. Over the years, many of the Independents in the House of Commons have been expelled from, or choose to leave, their party caucus. In this role independents have sometimes held the balance of power (e.g. Chuck Cadman and John Nunziata), but not many MPs are elected as independents.

To run for a seat in the House, candidates must file nomination papers bearing the signatures of at least fifty or one hundred constituents (depending on the size of the electoral district).

An individual must be an eligible voter (adult and a citizen), as of the day on which he or she is nominated, in order to stand as a candidate.

If you like public policy and people, then you have a good chance of having a fulfilling career as an MP. The role is very demanding and hard on family life. My wife remained in Toronto when I was in Ottawa except for some special occasions and events in the capital, so for one hundred and thirty days of the year we communicated by telephone. Apart from the summer recesses, work days were long and punishing. In Ottawa my typical day began at 6 a.m. and I returned to my duplex at nine p.m. to watch the news and go to bed. Returning to my riding on a Thursday or Friday evening, I typically faced three to four events each weekend–from cutting ribbons, to attending community fairs and other events. Then it was back on the plane Monday morning to Ottawa to jump back on that treadmill. On a more positive note, I found the work of an MP to be very stimulating and interesting, and I enormously appreciated the opportunity to engage in discussion and debate on a variety of public policy questions, and to meet and engage with world leaders and leaders in our country on a regular basis. In addition, solving problems for my constituents, and seeing the resultant joy on their faces, was one of the most rewarding experiences one can imagine.

Those elected to the House of Commons come from all walks of life – former teachers, radio announcers, lawyers, small business owners, and many more. They arrive in Ottawa with no training on how to perform as an MP. Learning mostly comes on—the—job. True, there are orientation sessions for new Parliamentarians, but they are focused mostly on bread and butter issues. How to hire staff; what one's budget is; how the shuttle bus service operates on the hill; how to order equipment, stationery, etc;—these are important issues for a novice on the Hill and they need to be dealt with. What is lacking, however, is information on the role and responsibilities of an MP. There should be more offered to new MPs in the following areas since these are matters which MPs deal with on a regular basis –

- difference between private members' business and government business;
- voting procedures in the Chamber;
- standing committee selection process;
- confidence votes – role of the Whips;
- holding the government to account through the estimates process, in the Chamber and in Committee;
- purpose of Standing Committees and a description of all of them;
- rules for speeches in the Chamber;
- how to table a motion or private members' bill in the House;
- house procedures and rules (e.g. quorum, 1st, 2nd and 3rd readings of Bills, closure, etc);
- how to table a petition, make a statement in the House, ask a question during Question Period;
- how to place a question on the order paper;
- how to make an access to information request;
- rules of decorum in the Chamber and at Committee;
- how to request an adjournment motion;
- the process for making an amendment to a Bill in Committee or in the Chamber;
- translation and Hansard services available;
- various parliamentary associations;
- etc., etc.

This list could go on and on and I don't recall being briefed, except in a very cursory way, on these topics when I arrived in Ottawa to take up my duties as an MP. Just before the 2008 general election, a Conservative Party colleague of mine in the House of Commons, John Williams, and I were having discussions with Treasury Board officials and representatives from the Canada School of Public Service about establishing training and educational programs for newly elected MPs with a curriculum that would address the topics above and other matters. With the election call, however, and with both John Williams and me not seeking re—election in 2008, this initiative will have to be taken up by others.

In 2010, at the federal level, Canada tied with Mauritania for 50th place for the number of women in our national parliament - with women representing 22.1% of Members of Parliament in the House of Commons (lower house), and 34.4% of Senators (upper house).

WOMEN IN NATIONAL PARLIAMENTS - World Averages

Total MPs	44,651
Gender breakdown known for	43,852
Men	35,446
Women	8,406
Percentage of women	19.2%

Single House or Lower House		Upper House or Senate	
Total MPs	37'790	Total MPs	6'861
Gender breakdown known for	37'021	Gender breakdown known for	6'861
Men	29'865	Men	5'581
Women	7'156	Women	1'250
Percentage of women	19.3%	Percentage of women	18.3%

Sixty-nine women were elected to the House of Commons in the 2008 general election in Canada – a record for our country. However, this represents just 22 per cent of the 308 total MPs, and only a modest gain over the 65 women in the 39th Canadian Parliament - so more needs to be done to encourage women to run for parliament, and to support their efforts to do so.

The number of women elected for each party, and the proportion of women in the party's elected caucus in the 40th Parliament, are as follows:

- Bloc Québecois - 15   (30.6% of caucus)
- Conservative - 23   (16.1% of caucus)
- Liberal - 19   (24.7% of caucus)
- NDP - 12   (32.4% of caucus)

In Canada's Senate, currently 32 of 93 seats are women, or 34.4%. In the 2008 election the Liberal Party of Canada ran a record number of female candidates, surpassing the NDP for the first time. The party fielded 113 women in 307 federal ridings, which means 36.9 per cent of Liberal candidates were female – making good on Stéphane Dion's promise that at least one-third of his candidates would be women.

I would like to see more women in the House of Commons to more adequately reflect the proportion of women in the general population. It is my view that women add to the general level of decorum in the House, and they bring a much-needed dimension to the policy and political debates.

As an MP, one is bombarded with a plethora of issues–pensions, the war in Afghanistan, employment insurance, immigration problems, taxation, climate change, access to capital for small businesses, expanding international markets for Canadian business, trade disputes with the U.S.A., same sex marriages, euthanasia, gun registration, violent crime, drugs, aboriginal governance and poverty, the homeless–to name but a few. One realizes that it is impossible to adequately cover all issues in depth and in a comprehensive way. There are just not enough hours in each day. One has to develop a focus on those issues that are particularly important to you and your constituents, and where you believe you can add some value to the discussion and debate. In my case, I decided early on that, given my business experience and my financial background and training, my emphasis would be placed on economic issues. To address the unfortunate level of violent crime occurring in my riding, I needed also to become very familiar with the *Criminal Code of Canada*, together with the socio—economic factors underlying this type of destructive behaviour.

While it is important to specialize, an MP needs to have a general understanding of all of the matters that are important to Canadians and which come before Parliament. If one of your constituents asks you about federal funding for autism, or coastal fishing quotas, or Veteran's benefits, or human rights in China, or aboriginal schooling and healthcare, or, or.........; it is not sufficient to say that one of your colleagues handles these issues for your party. You have to be able to come up with some answers – which will undoubtedly involve speaking with a relevant minister, or your opposition shadow cabinet minister or critic, for their insights and views on the topic under consideration. An MP must have a general knowledge of a vast array of matters under federal jurisdiction and some of this develops over time as you gain more experience. In that context, I recall an incident in a supermarket in my riding some years ago when a constituent recognized me and approached me to ask why a certain prisoner had been let out on parole! While it is not necessary to know the status of all prisoners in federal prisons, one never knows where the next challenge will come from–and you had better be ready.

Having said that, one needs to develop a focus and specialize in certain subject areas. In circa 2000, John Williams, a Conservative colleague of mine in the House of Commons, approached me and asked me if I would join the Global Organization of Parliamentarians Against Corruption (GOPAC) to fight the scourge of corruption and money laundering. I agreed to join him and his colleagues and I have been actively involved in this venture since. I had always been troubled by the scale and scope of global corruption, especially in the developing world, and how it was inhibiting our ability to lift people out of poverty.

GOPAC was largely a Canadian invention–and much of the initiative and credit goes to John Williams. The organization grew out of a frustration by John and a few others over a lack of focus on fighting corruption and the failure to act and follow—up after meeting after meeting on this topic.

GOPAC is an international network of parliamentarians dedicated to good governance and combating corruption throughout the world. In 2010 membership in the organization numbered nine hundred with representation in over 90 countries in all the regions of the world.

GOPAC was formally constituted in October 2002 as a result of conference in Ottawa which brought together over 170 parliamentarians and 400 observers dedicated to fighting corruption and improving good governance. It became a legal entity in the fall of 2003 – a not for profit under Canadian law.

We decided that political correctness in the approach to corruption was dysfunctional and not worthy of support. James Wolfensohn, on becoming President of the World Bank in July 1995, to his credit, took on the problem of global corruption and its impact on development assistance. Under his leadership, no more would corruption be referred to in World Bank documents as 'implicit taxes' or 'rent seeking behavior'. Like Wolfensohn, we at GOPAC 'call a spade a spade' and have no difficulty tackling the problem of corruption head on.

I am now on the Board of Directors of GOPAC, serving as Treasurer and as leader of the Global Task Force on Money Laundering. In these roles I speak out everywhere I can on the urgent need to 'think outside the box' in the fight against global corruption and money laundering. My participation in GOPAC led me to write a book, *The Poverty of Corrupt Nations*, in which I outline the scale and scope of global corruption and money laundering, and then I describe a Twenty Point Plan of attack.

***

I am often asked what motivated me to run for a seat in the House of Commons. In 1996, I was fifty years old and an opportunity presented itself to me to run. I concluded that it was going to be then or never. So after consulting with my wife and others, I decided to take the plunge. At that point I was steeped in politics and public policy, and those experiences were coursing through my veins. I thought it would be a demanding but a great experience to represent my country in the House of Commons, and I was motivated by a desire, perhaps immodestly, to add value to the debates. In 1996, when I first decided to run, unemployment was at a level of 11%—12% and I felt that given my business experience I might be able to assist in wrestling this number down. Also, because I was born and raised in Montreal, spoke some French, had lived on the west coast of Canada and later in Toronto, and had spent six years working and living abroad in Bermuda and later in South Africa, I believed and hoped that I could bring some unique perspectives and energy to the national unity discussion. So, I ran, and the rest is history, even if it is a small and modest slice.

In 2008 I decided that after five election campaigns and twelve and one half years in the House of Commons, I would not run in the October 2008 election. It was a tough decision in one sense because it had been a great run and I had really enjoyed the experience. I felt that I had made a difference in the lives of Canadians but that it was time to move on.

Having retired, or semi—retired, to Victoria, I do a modest amount of consulting/lobbying work with companies/organizations wishing to change laws or regulations in Ottawa, or anxious for things to remain the same. For causes I believe in, I am happy to assist those who need assistance in maneuvering through the maze of government departments and political apparatus on the hill to ensure, at least, that their voice is heard and understood. After that it is the politicians who must decide what is best for our country. To represent such entities in this way required that I register with the Office of the Commissioner of Lobbying of Canada. The Commissioner interprets and enforces the *Lobbyists Registration Act*, the *Lobbyists Registration Regulations* and the *Lobbyists' Code of Conduct.*

As an MP I would meet from time—to—time with lobbyists, usually with their client and I had no difficulty with that. They would present their case to me, I would listen, ask questions; and as long as one realizes that there is more than one side to a story, the system works as it is supposed to. I had no difficulty, nor do I have today any problem with the registration and regulation of lobbyists. Total transparency is a tenet that I have always subscribed to.

The *Lobbyists' Code of Conduct* is designed to ensure that lobbying is done ethically and to the highest standards so that government decision—making is seen as objective, impartial and honest.

Lobbyists are defined as those who are paid to communicate with federal public office holders about pending or finalized government decisions. Lobbyists are required to register with the Lobbyist Registration Branch and when making a representation to a Designated Public Office Holder (DPOH), disclose the identity of the person or organization on whose behalf the representation is made, as well as the reasons for the approach.

Monthly returns, describing any oral and arranged communications with Designated Public Office Holders (DPOH) must be filed by lobbyists. This information is completely transparent and easily accessed through the web site of the Office of the Commissioner of Lobbying of Canada.

Designated Public Office Holders are defined as follows —

"The *Lobbying Act* defines designated public office holder (DPOH) as "ministers, ministerial staff, deputy ministers and chief executives of departments, officials in departments at the rank of associate deputy minister or assistant deputy minister, as well as those occupying positions of comparable rank". For the purposes of the Act, 'departments' includes those federal departments and agencies listed in Schedules 1, 1.1, and 2 of the *Financial Administration Act*. The *Lobbying Act* further defines "any person identified by the Prime Minister as having had the task of providing advice and support to him or her during the transition period leading up to the swearing in of the Prime Minister and his or her ministry", as being subject to the *Lobbying Act* as if they were a DPOH"[2].

An additional eleven positions or classes of positions have been designated as DPOH by way of regulation including the Chief of the Defense Staff (Canadian Forces), the Comptroller General of Canada, and the Judge Advocate General (Canadian Forces).

I think it is important for Canadians to know who is speaking with Ottawa's decision—makers. The Lobbyist Registration system works and I fully support it.

---

2   Office of the Commissioner of Lobbying of Canada web site.

Making Laws and Other Moments in Ottawa

While there is no such thing as a typical week for an MP in Ottawa when the House is in session, allow me to paint a few brush strokes to give an idea of how MPs spend their time.

What one does on Parliament Hill depends to some extent on what roles and responsibilities have been assigned to you. Of course the prime minister and his/her ministers form the cabinet and have the major responsibility of running the government. Parliament passes laws, and the government is held to account on behalf of Canadians by the leader of the official opposition, other opposition leaders, and parliament as a whole. Standing committees are established by parliament to review legislation and report to parliament with recommendations on matters they have studied. Parliamentary secretaries support the work of ministers – especially in the House of Commons and in committee. As parliamentary secretary I would attend numerous briefings on new legislation and on parliamentary tactics; prepare for Question Period and standing committee meetings; work on speeches and then deliver them; participate in meetings with the minister and the department; and work on specific projects that the minister has assigned to you—very often issues raised by the government caucus requiring a solution. These tasks on their own can be very time consuming in addition to one's own responsibilities as an MP. As parliamentary secretary, no additional staff resources were assigned to me; however both Paul Martin and Anne McLellan named a dedicated staff person in their minister's office to work with me exclusively. Other ministerial staff were available to me on an as needed basis—especially the

Minister's Assistant on Parliamentary Affairs. Officials in the department were available to me on call and they were very helpful and responsive. Notwithstanding these supports, the workload was considerable – but at the same time interesting and challenging.

When bills originating from one's portfolio as parliamentary secretary (PS) are being debated in the House of Commons, it is the PS's responsibility to steer and coordinate the debate and assist caucus colleagues in that process. This typically involves leading off the debate on the bill in the Chamber; offering to provide speaking points for colleagues; actively engaging with questions and comments after opposition party members have made their speeches (and providing 'cannon fodder' to colleagues for their rebuttals to opposition attacks on the bill). Departmental officials are available in the government lobby–a short step away to answer any technical questions you might have as the debate evolves. The parliamentary secretary is also the lead on proposed amendments, and on the advice from staff from the whip's office, provides guidance to caucus colleagues on procedural and substantive votes on the bill as it progresses through the House. The reality is that when bills emanating from your department are in the chamber or at committee, the parliamentary secretary must be present full time to steer the bill's passage.

Chairing a standing committee demands a great deal of time working with the members of the committee, the committee steering committee, the committee clerk and the committee research assistants. Bills need to be dealt with expeditiously, meetings chaired usually twice per week, witnesses called, and reports drafted and tabled in the House. As Chair of the House of Commons Standing Committee on Finance, we traveled across the country each year in advance of the budget and scheduled pre—budget consultation meetings in all major centres across Canada. Sometimes the committee would split up – one group traveling to eastern Canada and the other to western Canada; but regardless, this activity, albeit important, took two—three weeks to complete including negotiating over drafts of the report that would eventually be tabled in parliament and reviewed carefully by the Finance Minister as he developed his budget.

Chairing a caucus committee, like the Ontario Liberal Caucus which I chaired for one year, can be very time consuming. In 1998/99 the Ontario Liberal caucus was about 130 members strong, including 101 MPs and about 30 Ontario Senators. It was a large caucus and chairing this group was a demanding job preparing for the meetings Wednesday mornings from 9 a.m. – 10 a.m., chairing the actual meeting, and then shortly after

10 a.m. delivering my report to the full national Caucus when I would raise the important issues of the day from the perspective of the Ontario caucus for the attention of the prime minister, cabinet ministers and the balance of the national caucus. During that period, the Ontario caucus executive, which included all the regional chairs (Greater Toronto, Eastern Ontario, Northern Ontario, South West Ontario, etc.) would meet Tuesday in the late afternoon before votes. At these meetings various Ontario stakeholder groups would present briefs to our executive and we would summarize the results of these meetings for the members as a whole.

Barring these additional responsibilities, Monday mornings would start with a 7 a.m. flight from Toronto to Ottawa. After dropping off my bag at my apartment, I would proceed to my hill office and meet with my staff for up to an hour discussing the week's program and agendas. After dealing with some correspondence and phone calls, it was off to the House of Commons Chamber for House Duty. When on the House Duty Roster, usually 2—3 times per week in 3 hour units each, it was one's responsibility to be in the Chamber to ensure that quorum was reached (twenty MPs overall in the Chamber), to participate in debates, and to be present to vote on motions and other procedural ploys. Participation on two Standing Committees would require attendance at four meetings per week (e.g. Tuesday and Thursday mornings and afternoons). Caucus meetings take care of Wednesday mornings and Question Period and Statements by Members consumed one hour per day. Filling in the gaps in time would be meetings with constituents, non—governmental organizations (NGOs), special interest groups, Ministers and other colleagues on a variety of issues, debating bills in the House outside of House Duty, French language instruction, meeting with staff to review a range of matters including plans for any upcoming travel.

How does an MP participate in the debate in the House on a Bill that she/he is interested in? Is it solely a matter of catching the attention of the Speaker and rising in one's place in the House? Well fortunately, or unfortunately depending on one's point—of—view, the debating process on bills and motions is somewhat more organized, although opportunities to participate in debates are numerous and largely unrestricted.

Before votes are called in the Chamber or in committee on bills or motions, all debate must be exhausted and the debate deemed to have 'collapsed'. At that point, the speaker will 'put the question' to those present in the Chamber, and a vote will be called, or deferred to a future sitting of the House with the prior agreement of the party whips.

All MPs wishing to speak to a bill are able to unless the available time for debate has been limited by a closure or time allocation motion adopted by the House. Closure or time allocation motions are very contentious and always contested by opposition MPs. For this reason they are tools, however unpopular, available only to majority governments, who are able to force an affirmative vote through the House. This type of procedure invariably invites criticism that debate is being stifled, and democracy denied.

Speaking in the House of Commons

Baring closure or time allocation restrictions, lists are drawn up by the party whips of those MPs wishing to participate in the debate, and these lists, in sequential order, are provided to the speaker. The speaker then works off these lists and rotates the speaking opportunities amongst all of the parties, and independent MPs. First comes a government MP, if the bill is a government bill, followed by an MP from the official opposition, followed next by a Bloc Québécois MP, followed by an NDP MP, followed by an independent MP, and then the process repeats itself–government MP, official opposition MP, etc.—until the debate is exhausted and all of those MPs wishing to enter the debate have had an opportunity to do so. While the speaker has a list of identified MPs wishing to speak to the bill, that MP must be present in the Chamber, and rise to be recognized by the speaker when it is his/her turn – otherwise the speaker will turn to the next MP on the agreed—to list.

If the bill or motion is considered Private Member's business, the proponent of the bill or motion is the first to speak followed by a government MP, and then other MPs in the same rotation as for government bills. Time in the Chamber for Private Member's business is, however, limited— usually to three hours in total for each bill or motion, or one hour each for 1st, 2nd, and 3rd readings.

The length of speeches is defined by the rules of the House. Lead off speeches typically have no time restrictions, followed by twenty minute speeches and then ten minutes of questions and comments. Very often, twenty minute speeches are shared by two caucus colleagues so that each MP has ten minutes to speak and five minutes for questions and comments. After a stipulated number of speeches, the Speaker, on the recommendation of the party whips, may limit the opportunities for questions and comments and then one speech follows another. Speeches on private members business follow similar rules, although apart from the proponent, questions and comments on speeches are not provided for.

There is no formal structure for participation in the questions and comments portion of the debate. MPs who wish to comment must rise in their place following a speech and the Speaker will recognize the first to do so. This is followed by a rotation of the debaters amongst the parties—with the time restricted to leave time for a response.

While the above description for debate on government bills is technically how the process works, in reality there is much negotiation and 'horse trading' amongst party whips on how much time will be available for debates on specific bills in the Chamber. These negotiated deals can only go so far however. The speaker is obliged to recognize any MP who rises in their place to debate a bill – unless closure or time allocation has been invoked. An MP may decide, notwithstanding any advice from their party whip and informal agreements in place, that they wish to debate a bill and nothing prevents them from doing so.

If the government whip, for example, would like to expedite the debate on a government bill and deal with it in say three days, opposition party whips may agree to this, to the extent that they can control this, but they would seek something in return. The opposition party whip might agree with the three day scenario conditional on the government bringing another government bill before the Chamber within one week; or delaying the introduction of another government bill for three weeks, etc., etc. This is where the negotiation occurs and where tentative deals are struck. Again, not all MPs feel bound by informal arrangements entered into by party whips—but usually some discipline prevails.

The government side is often conflicted in balancing the desire to process bills expeditiously, and the need for government MPs to argue the government's position on bills before the House. Because speeches on bills are rotated amongst all parties, the government could ask its MPs, after some of its members have spoken, to cease and desist future debate on the bill. What this means, however, is that all the time in the Chamber will be taken up with opposition party MPs criticizing the Bill and poking holes in the legislation–with no opportunity for rebuttal or defence by government members. The end result is that government MPs usually enter the fray and try to correct the impressions left by opposition colleagues–thereby extending the debating time on the Bill.

It is possible to get a lot of work done when sitting in the Chamber of the House of Commons – either at one's desk or alternatively in the House lobby. There is a lobby for members on the government side adjacent to the Chamber and a lobby for members of the opposition on the other side of the Chamber. Members can move freely back and forth into the lobby and back to the Chamber. In the lobbies there is continuous TV coverage of the debates and procedures in the Chamber. Staff from the party whips' offices monitor developments closely and from time—to—time will call members back into the Chamber for a quorum call, to vote on a procedural motion, or to vote on a bill. Likewise, MPs monitor the debates and should they wish to enter the debate they will re—enter the Chamber and try and get the attention of the Speaker.

In the meantime, the lobby is a great place to make phone calls, have meetings, do some reading and paperwork, and to chat about politics with colleagues. A buffet lunch is served around noon each day in the lobbies so that MPs can stay close to the Chamber. This is typically a hot lunch of fish and chips, spaghetti, meat and potatoes, or other delicacy, accompanied by soup, salad and dessert and tea or coffee. There have been complaints registered from time—to—time by MPs about the quality of the food or pleas for a healthier menu, but while some changes are made the menu doesn't seem to have been altered to any great degree over the years.

If the numbers in the Chamber are respectable it is possible to head up to the Parliamentary Restaurant where the ambiance and food choices are much better. I tended to do this if a constituent was in town, or if I needed to meet with someone during the lunch period. Before departing, I would check in with the staff member of our Whip's office seated in the lobby to see if it was possible to leave and to ensure that if I was needed in the Chamber, I could be reached in a hurry.

When I first arrived in Ottawa, the Greater Toronto Area (GTA) Liberal Party caucus met every Tuesday evening after votes – from around 7 p.m. sometimes until 10 p.m. Pizza would be brought in, and a range of issues affecting the Toronto area would be vigorously discussed and debated. At that time the GTA Caucus numbered about thirty—five members and so the discussion was usually lively and protracted.

Unless I had house duty on Friday or other responsibilities in Ottawa, I would fly back to Toronto on Thursday evening. When I served as parliamentary secretary, often Fridays were spent in Ottawa substituting for ministers Martin or McLellan as they travelled to their constituencies, or to conduct other government business outside of the nation's capital. Question Period (QP) is conducted each sitting day of the House at 2:15 p.m., Monday to Thursday, and at 11:15 a.m. on Fridays.

After QP I would travel to Toronto and over the weekend attend a few political functions and then it was back to Ottawa again on Monday morning.

If I was able to travel back to Toronto on Thursday evening, I would have meetings with constituents, and sometimes other interested parties, all day on Friday at my constituency office, starting at 8:30 a.m. and finishing at 5 p.m. or later. On these days there could also be local factory tours, ribbon—cutting events, and other functions mixed in and around the office meetings.

My constituency, which has a large South Asian population, is home to many Indian restaurants and food shops. One day, I ventured into one of them, as I often do, to purchase some samosas and naan bread. The owner of the shop recognized me as the local member of parliament. "Aren't you the local M.P.?" he asked. We shook hands and introduced ourselves. "I am amazed that you would come into my shop," he remarked. "Why so?" I responded—puzzled by his comment. "In India," he said, "a member of parliament would probably not enter such modest premises; but, if they did, it would undoubtedly be with two or three bodyguards!" I guess if you live by graft and corruption, you make friends and enemies and you need protection from the latter"[3]. "I guess if you live by graft and corruption, you make friends and enemies and you need protection from the latter"[3].

The decision—making process in Ottawa is somewhat complicated and sometimes convoluted. Decisions made on parliament hill involve a number of complex interactions amongst a variety of players including the government caucus, cabinet ministers, the prime minister, the prime minister's office staff (PMO), ministerial staff, the caucus research bureau, the House of Commons and its standing committees, the media, pollsters, and others.

Some decisions are 'top down' in the sense that ministers and the prime minister, based often on advice from the bureaucracy, or from stakeholder groups. Other decisions flow from views expressed by caucus based on what they are hearing from their constituents. Prime Minister Chrétien always listened carefully to the views of caucus during the Wednesday morning meetings, and he conveyed the message to us that this was the most important advice he received. I believe he meant it.

Time spent by members of parliament in the House of Commons is predominately to debate and process bills, which are in effect proposed laws. Most of the bills are government bills but one hour each day is reserved to consider private member's bills or motions. I will outline later what bills and motions are, and provide some examples.

Given the bilingual nature of Canada, our parliament is conducted in both official languages – English and French. Simultaneous translation occurs during all the debates and business that occurs in the Chambers of the House of Commons and Senate, and also at all committee meetings, and at all caucus meetings, with the exception perhaps of the Bloc Québécois caucus meetings. Press conferences on the hill are typically conducted in both languages.

Individualized one—on—one French or English language instruction is available virtually on demand–the challenge is finding the time to do it. For the first few years of my time in Ottawa, I instructed my staff to find the time to schedule one half hour of French language training with my capable and affable instructor Pierre Beauchamp each and every week when I was on the hill. During summer recesses, I also organized three separate one week intensive language training tutorials – two in Québec City and one in Chicoutimi. The latter experience, in the Lac St. Jean Region of Québec, studying with my instructor at l'Université du Québec

---

3   Roy Cullen, The Poverty of Corrupt Nations, Blue Butterfly Book Publishing Inc., Toronto, Canada, 2008, page 45

à Chicoutimi, and living in with a local unilingual Francophone family, had me thinking in the French language when I left Chicoutimi after my one week session.

Out of respect for French—speaking Canadians, when speaking in the House of Commons and at standing committee meetings I always spoke some French whenever possible. If I was delivering a prepared speech in the House of Commons, about twenty percent of the content would be in French. Sometimes this involved having selected parts of the speech translated by the House of Commons translation staff – another efficient service that was readily available. If I was delivering a speech on behalf of a minister, I would ask the department to incorporate both languages into my text. Even during Question Period, if responding to a question from the Bloc Québécois, I would do my best to deliver the first sentence or two in French without getting into too much trouble.

The Parliament of Canada web site succinctly describes how Bills are processed–

"A Cabinet Minister or backbench Member proposing a bill first moves for the House's 'leave' to introduce it. This is given automatically and without debate or vote. Next comes the motion that the bill be read a first time and printed. This also is automatic and without debate or vote. On a later day comes the motion for second reading. This is the stage at which Members debate the principle of the bill. If it passes second reading, it goes to a committee of the House, usually a standing committee. Each such committee may hear witnesses, and considers the bill, clause by clause, before reporting it (with or without amendments) back to the House. The size of these committees varies from parliament to parliament, but the parties are represented in proportion to their strength in the House itself. Some bills, such as appropriation bills (based on the Estimates), which seek to withdraw money from the Consolidated Revenue Fund, are dealt with by the whole House acting as a committee.

Committees, sitting under less formal rules than the House, examine bills clause by clause. Each clause has to be passed. Any member of the committee can move amendments. When all the clauses have been dealt with, the chairperson reports the bill to the House with any amendments that have been adopted.

When a committee has reported the bill to the House, Members at this "report stage" may move amendments to the various clauses (usually, amendments they have not had the opportunity to propose in committee). When these have been passed, or rejected, the bill goes to third reading. If the motion for third reading carries, the bill goes to the Senate, where it goes through much the same process. Bills initiated in the Senate and passed there come to the Commons, and go through the same stages as Commons bills. No bill can become law (become an Act) unless it has been passed in identical form by both Houses and has been assented to, in the Queen's name, by the Governor General or a deputy of the Governor General (usually a Supreme Court judge). Assent has never been refused to a federal bill, and our first Prime Minister declared roundly that refusal was obsolete and had become unconstitutional. In Britain, Royal Assent has never been refused since 1707.

There are about twenty standing committees (Agriculture and Agri—food, Canadian Heritage, Transport, and so on) whose members are appointed at the beginning of each session or in September of each year, to oversee the work of government departments, to review particular areas of federal policy, to exercise procedural and administrative responsibilities related to Parliament, to consider matters referred to them by the House, and to report their findings and proposals to the House for its consideration.

Included in the work of standing committees is the consideration of the government's spending estimates. The Standing Orders provide for these estimates to be sent to the committees for review.

Finally, standing committees are designated as having certain matters permanently referred to them (such as reports tabled in the House pursuant to a statute, and the annual report of certain Crown corporations). Each of these automatic Orders of Reference is permanently before the committees, and may be considered and reported on as the committees deem appropriate.

The House of Commons can, and does, set up special committees for the examination of particular subjects, including legislative committees whose mandate is solely to examine a particular piece of legislation. It also establishes, with the Senate, joint committees of the two Houses".[4]

The full list of House of Commons Standing Committees, as of 2009 (40th Parliament, 2nd Session), is as follows –
  • Aboriginal Affairs and Northern Development
  • Access to Information, Privacy and Ethics
  • Agriculture and Agri—Food
  • Canadian Heritage
  • Citizenship and Immigration
  • Environment and Sustainable Development
  • Finance
  • Fisheries and Oceans

---

4   Parliament of Canada web site, *What Goes on in Parliament.*

- Foreign Affairs and International Development
- Government Operations and Estimates
- Health
- Human Resources, Social Development and the Status of Persons with Disabilities
- Industry, Science and Technology
- International Trade
- Justice and Human Rights
- Liaison Committee
- National Defense
- Natural Resources
- Official Languages
- Procedure and House Affairs
- Public Accounts
- Public Safety and National Security
- Status of Women
- Transport, Infrastructure and Communities
- Veterans Affairs

Currently there are two special standing committees –
- Special Committee on the Canadian Mission in Afghanistan; and,
- Bill C – 31 *An Act to amend the Canada Elections Act and the Public Service Employment Act*

The Senate Standing Committees are configured differently –
- Aboriginal Peoples
- Aging (Special)
- Agriculture and Forestry
- Banking, Trade and Commerce
- Conflict of Interest for Senators
- Energy, the Environment and Natural Resources
- Fisheries and Oceans
- Foreign Affairs and International Trade
- Human Rights
- Internal Economy, Budgets and Administration
- Legal and Constitutional Affairs
- National Finance
- National Security and Defense

- Subcommittee Veterans Affairs
- Official Languages
- Rules, Procedures and the Rights of Parliament
- Selection Committee
- Social Affairs, Science and Technology
- Subcommittee on Cities
- Subcommittee on Population Health
- Transport and Communications

The ability of an MP to have his or her private members' bill or motion debated and passed, depend on where they are placed in the order of precedence which is established at the start of each session of the House of Commons.

Establishing List and order of precedence at beginning of session.

> **87. (1)(a)(i)** *At the beginning of the first session of a Parliament, the Clerk of the House, acting on behalf of the Speaker, shall, after notifying all Members of the time, date and place, conduct a random draw of the names of all Members of the House to establish the List for the Consideration of Private Members' Business, and, on the twentieth sitting day following the draw, the first thirty names on the List shall, subject to paragraph (c) of this Standing Order, constitute the order of precedence.*[5]

Members of Parliament debate government bills and also private members' bills and motions. The average number of bills introduced by MPs has averaged about 280 per session in the last few years. On average, 90 MPs introduce bills each session averaging approximately 3 bills for each participating MP. Five hours are set aside each week for the House of Commons to debate and vote upon private members business.

During a session, the Order of Precedence is replenished whenever less than fifteen items remain on the Order of Precedence by adding items from the next fifteen members on the list for the consideration of private members' business who have introduced a bill or given notice of a motion.

A session of a parliament begins following an election, or after a speech from the throne, and ends with the prorogation of parliament by the

---

5   Standing Orders of the House of Commons, June 2009

Governor General, on the advice of the prime minister. Most unfinished business dies and committees cease to function. Parliament then stands prorogued until the opening of the next session on a specified date. This date may be changed by a further proclamation.

Government bills that have not received Royal Assent prior to prorogation can be reinstated in the next session only if the House takes a decision to this effect. All items of private members' business are automatically reinstated. Tabling of documents before the House must await the beginning of the new session. Requests for responses to petitions and for the production of papers remain in effect, as do requests made for government responses to committee reports.

Prime Minister Stephen Harper's decision to prorogue Parliament in 2008 and then again in 2009 is unprecedented and attracted the wrath of Canadians. The 2008 Prorogation was clearly requested (and sanctioned by Governor General Michaëlle Jean) so that the Conservative government could avoid a confidence vote that it was sure to lose – forcing an election that Canadians did not want. The only similar prorogation in Canada occurred in 1873 when Prime Minister Sir John A. Macdonald asked Governor General Lord Dufferin to prorogue parliament in order to stop the work of a committee investigating MacDonald's involvement in the Pacific Scandal. While the Governor General did reluctantly prorogue parliament, he limited it to a period of ten weeks. When parliament returned, Macdonald was censured and had to resign.

The reason behind the prorogation request by Prime Minister Harper in 2009 is more complex. The Conservative government rationalized the move on the basis of a need to 'refresh' its agenda and come forward with a Speech from the Throne in March 2009. With Canada hosting the 2010 Winter Olympics in February, the Conservative government argued that Canadians will be focused on the Olympic Games and more ready to focus on Parliament once they are over.

In my judgment, these reasons cited are purely rationalizations to mask the real reasons for the prorogation which were –

- to restructure the Senate Committees and take full advantage of the newly acquired Conservative majority in the Senate;
- to avoid the discomfort of further enquiries over the handling of Taliban prisoners in Afghanistan; and
- to force a vote of confidence in the House of Commons in March 2010 on a new budget leading (hopefully for Conservatives!) to a majority government.

It would appear that the prorogation strategy backfired. Canadians, rightly so, wondered why the Conservative Government needed to 'refresh' its agenda when there was still a backlog of legislation in parliament to deal with. They saw the prime minister's moves as further examples of his disrespect for parliament.

Dissolution, for an election, ends the life of a Parliament; the last session of a Parliament is therefore the one that ends with dissolution. The proclamation (issued by the Governor General on the advice of the Prime Minister) dissolving a Parliament is usually followed by others, fixing the date of a general election and summoning the new Parliament to meet on a specific date.

Dissolution brings to an end all Chamber activity and all business before both Houses. All committees cease to exist and requests for Government responses to committee reports lapse. The Speaker and several of the other elected officers of Parliament continue to perform certain administrative functions until they are replaced or re—elected in a new Parliament following a general election.

Some of my colleagues in the House became very conversant with the rules of procedure – Paul Szabo and Derek Lee come to mind. I was not so interested in mastering the rules and processes of the House, but rather the substantive issues being debated, but one needs to know what the pitfalls are, and where the landmines might be, especially in carrying out the responsibilities of Parliamentary Secretary and in advancing one's own Private Member's Bill.

As an MP, every day can bring new surprises that end up requiring your immediate attention and forcing you to drop what you were doing beforehand.

The Senators hockey team in Ottawa was struggling financially through the late 1990's. On Jan 18th, 2000, Minister of Industry John Manley announced a plan to provide the team with a $20 million subsidy—and my phones, and my colleagues' phones, started ringing. The House of Commons was in recess at the time so I responded to my constituents' complaints from my constituency office. Over 50 people in my area had called my office to protest the subsidy to the NHL team. I stuck to my self—made policy that I responded to my constituents in the medium they chose. If they wrote to me, I replied by letter. If they sent me an e—mail, I e—mailed back. If they 'phoned' me, I called back; and if they wished to meet with me, that would be accommodated as soon as practically possible. So there I was, with 50 phone message slips asking me to call about the

John Manley bail out proposal. I sat down one morning and called them all back. These were difficult calls because I was not a fan of John Manley's idea, nor were any of the 50 constituents I spoke with that day. He was a colleague, a Minister, and we were the governing party at the time, so I mostly listened as people 'vented spleen'.

After the calls, which took up the entire morning and part of the afternoon, I instructed my Toronto office manager, Fran Watt, to draft a letter post haste for me to send to John Manley recommending that he rescind the Senator subsidy proposal. That evening, while attending a political reception in downtown Toronto, a Liberal colleague, Dennis Mills, pulled me aside and asked me what I was hearing about the hockey subsidy idea. Dennis had become the 'go to' person within our caucus on matters relating to sport. For many years he had chaired the House of Commons Subcommittee on the Study of Sport in Canada of the Standing Committee on Canadian Heritage. He had been responsible for a report entitled *Sport in Canada: Everybody's Business*. I told Dennis I was getting killed on this issue in my riding and that I would be communicating with John Manley to recommend he pull the plug on the subsidy.

Dennis whispered to me "Not to worry Roy, John has called a press conference for tomorrow morning, January 21st, at 10 am at which time he will announce that financial support for the Ottawa Senators will not be forthcoming from the federal government." I uttered a sigh of relief. Driving home that evening I pondered the politics of this. What was the point of a letter from me to John Manley <u>after</u> he announced that there would be no subsidy, I asked myself? I pulled my car over to the curbside, called my office manager, and asked her to have the draft letter to the Minister on my desk at 8:30 a.m. the next morning – ready for my signature. The next morning at 9 a.m., the signed letter, recommending that John Manley drop the subsidy proposal for the Senators, was faxed to the minister's office. At 10 am, as Dennis had predicted, Industry Minister Manley announced that the Government of Canada had withdrawn its $20 million offer to the NHL Senators. At that point I made a crass political decision and put the wheels in motion to send a letter to the 50 constituents who had contacted me in opposition to the hockey subsidy. The note simply thanked each of them for their input and drew their attention to the John Manley press release. I also attached a copy of my January 21st letter to John Manley. I didn't claim single—handed responsibility for the Manley pull back, or take any credit. The note to constituents simple addressed the facts–I left my constituents to reach their own conclusions. If, after reading this correspondence, they concluded that contacting their MP when they felt strongly about an issue was a useful thing to do, I would have accomplished my objective.

Too often I was told that Canadians who telephoned their Member of Parliament in many cases never had the courtesy of a return call. To me this was unforgiveable. I ran my offices differently. A case in point – a telephone message was handed to me one day from a female constituent who wished to speak to me about recent salary increases for MPs. I knew this conversation would not be a joyful experience but I 'girded my loins' and called her back. Apparently she and her friends had been playing bridge one day and were complaining about recently announced MP salary increases. They were angry because all four of them were living on fixed incomes and their indexed pensions had been increased more modestly than the MP salaries. They were all surviving on modest incomes and just making ends meet. One of the bridge players suggested they all call their MPs. Three of them refused on the grounds that their MP would never call them back. My constituent decided to call me. As it turned out, when she did, and after we conversed and as I struggled to justify our pay increase, a negative was converted into a positive experience. My constituent thanked me profusely for calling her back and she told me she was going to be claiming bragging rights when her bridge group next assembled!

Members of Parliament debate government bills and also private members' bills and motions. The average number of bills introduced by MPs has averaged about 280 per session, while the number of motions has averaged about 495 per session. On average, 90 MPs introduce bills each session, while about 85 MPs introduce motions. Five hours are set aside each week for the House of Commons to debate and vote upon Private members Business.

A motion is a proposal moved by one member in accordance with well—established rules that the House do something, or order something done or express an opinion with regard to some matter. A motion initiates a debate and gives rise to a vote by the House. Motions passed by parliament are not binding on the government, but the government of the day views them as expressions of the will of parliament.

Private members' motions are amendable and must be drafted in such a way as to enable the House to express agreement or disagreement with what is proposed. Such motions normally require written notice before they can be moved in the House.

For example, in 2004, I tabled the following somewhat convoluted Motion, which was subsequently defeated –

"That, in the opinion of this House, the government should negotiate an end to the harmful U.S. countervailing duty process that is crippling Canada's softwood lumber industry unjustly, by replacing this U.S. trade remedy process with one which either (a) focuses on net subsidies –taking into account the substantial manufacturing subsidies such as tax free bonds, sales tax abatements, property tax reductions, cheap industrial land, and favourable energy co—generation agreements—which are available at the U.S. state and local government level, or (b) focuses exclusively on whether or not policies in Canada, and elsewhere, are anti—competitive in nature (e.g. involving price fixing, price collusion or other anti—competitive behavior); and that in addition to (a) and (b) above the government launch a negotiation with the U.S. government to eliminate harmful tax competition, in particular manufacturing subsidies, that is occurring between Canada and the U.S.A".

The point I was trying to highlight is the hypocrisy of the Americans for attacking alleged subsidies to our Canadian forest product companies when US forestry companies are in fact the recipients of significant financial support from local, state, and federal governments in that country. Although the motion was defeated, it provided me with the opportunity to make my case in the House of Commons and other fora.

This motion went through a number of drafts before it complied with the rules of the House (e.g. no emotive language or judgmental comments, etc, allowed). A motion must also be contained in no more than one sentence, which explains why the motion rambles on, and on and....... on.

Twenty "Opposition Days" or "Supply Days" each calendar year are set aside in the House of Commons to provide opportunities for the opposition parties to focus the debate for one full day on a topic of their choosing. They are usually designed to criticize and embarrass the government. I recall one such motion which was tabled in the fall of 2000 by the Alliance Party. The motion proposed to eliminate the

1.5 cents per litre gasoline tax which was introduced by the Liberal government as a deficit reduction measure in 1995. By 2000 the federal deficit had been completely eliminated - making it difficult for the government to justify its continued existence. The nature and wording of opposition motions are only made known to the Speaker, the government and the House of Commons the day before the debate, so the lead time is minimal. The government of the day, and other opposition parties, scramble to formulate a position and debating points. On this occasion, I was serving as parliamentary secretary to finance minister Paul Martin and when this motion was tabled Minister Martin was preparing to leave the country the next day for an important international meeting with other finance ministers. We sat that evening in the Minister's office and discussed tactics before the Minister left on his trip. I was asked to work with my colleague , Dan McTeague, the MP from what is now Pickering-Scarborough East, and with the Minister's assistant Karl Littler, and develop a strong response to the motion. Dan was our caucus guru on gasoline and fuel pricing, and Karl was Paul Martin's trusted tax policy advisor. My first move was to meet with Dan later that evening to prepare for the full day debate the next day. Dan correctly pointed out that a 1.5 cent reduction in the gasoline tax would not find its way to consumers, but would be gobbled up by the oil companies in an afternoon. Gasoline prices moved quickly and wildly and there would be no way to ensure that the gas tax reduction would be passed on to vehicle owners. We decided instead to focus on relief for Canadians generally who soon would be facing a very cold winter and exceptionally high and rising prices heating oil. As an alternative to eliminating the 1.5 cent gas tax, Dan, Karl and I were of the view that Relief for Heating Expenditure (RHE) payments to low- and modest-income households would be a better alternative. This relief would flow directly to Canadians so they would immediately see the benefit. Time was of the essence because winter, and the 2000 election, was upon us. Late into the evening, following a sign off, we pulled together some materials, speeches and an amendment to the motion. Because of some savvy work by Dan during the debate the next day, we were able to table our amendment which left the door open for a heating expenditure rebate solution. Motions are not binding on the government but nonetheless success with this amendment was an important victory. In our government's October 2000 *Economic Statement and Budget Update*, we announced that the government would provide one-time relief to those eligible for the January 2001 payment of the goods and services tax credit (GSTC). The relief provided for heating expenses was $125 to individuals or $250 to families. The total cost of the relief for the year ended March 31, 2001 was over $1.4 billion and reached 8.6 million recipients. The vehicle of the goods and services tax credit was chosen to deliver the relief as a matter of expediency given the logistics of providing Canadians with help when they needed it most. Unfortunately, some of the payments, albeit a relatively small number, reached individuals who shouldn't have benefited – like prisoners in jail, student renters, and the like. This is what the media focused on and so regrettably the implementation of this measure became the central issue.

As an MP one has the opportunity to promote one's own ideas in the most important law and policy making institution in our country–the Parliament of Canada. It presents at the same time a burden of responsibility since you are able, with hard work and commitment, to influence national public policy. You want to be sure that what you are proposing makes sense and is good public policy for Canada.

As a self—confessed Canadian nationalist, during the 2000's, I became very concerned about the volume of foreign takeovers of Canadian icon companies. Beginning with the 1999 acquisition of MacMillan Bloedel Ltd. (MacBlo) by the U.S. giant Weyerhaeuser of Federal Way, Washington, the list of foreign takeovers of Canadian companies keeps growing and growing –

INCO
Falconbridge
IPSCO
Hudson's Bay
Dofasco
Algoma Steel
Fairmont Hotels
Labatt's
CN
Four Seasons Hotels

Energy and other natural resource companies are special targets of private equity players awash with cash, and by companies in emerging economies seeking more control over their commodity supply—chain.

I was shocked when, in 2004, China Minmetals Corporation, a state—owned enterprise in the Peoples Republic of China (PRC), attempted to acquire 100% of the outstanding common shares of Noranda Inc. – one of Canada's premier natural resource companies, and a company I had been associated with when I worked at Noranda Forest Inc.

I spoke out in the House of Commons, in caucus, and in the media against this acquisition. Thankfully, the PRC company backed away from this deal, but I wondered at the time if this was a case of 'first time lucky'. When in Beijing with Prime Minister Martin in 2005, a group of us made a visit to the Communist Party External Affairs Office (surprisingly, a large high rise building devoted solely to external matters!) and I raised the question of state—owned enterprises in the PRC generally, and specifically the China Minmetals attempt to takeover Noranda. We were told that while the PRC was in the process of privatizing many of these corporations in China, the large natural resource companies would remain under the control of their government because of the significant contribution they made to government revenues. I wondered at the time what the Chinese reaction would be if a Canadian corporation tried to acquire a strategically important PRC company, but I already knew the answer would be a resounding NO.

Just prior to Inco being acquired in 2006 by Vale, a Brazilian mining company; and Falconbridge being swallowed -up by the Swiss-based mining company Xstrata, I spoke to Hon. Maxime Bernier, who was Minister of Industry at that time, in the House of Commons. I asked him, to no avail, to delay the decision of his review by the Competition Bureau of the Vale and Xstrata takeovers to allow more time for a *Made-in-Canada* solution – like an Inco/Falconbridge merger. The EU State Commission for the Protection of Economic Competition had taken months to arrive at their decision on these takeovers, but for some reason the Minister of Industry was anxious to come to a hasty conclusion.

Since the *Investment Canada Act* was passed in 1985, there have been over 11,000 foreign acquisitions of Canadian companies! No investments have ever been blocked under the *Investment Canada Act*, with the exception of the MacDonald Dettwiler & Associates sale in 2008!

In a December 2007 twelve page brief that I submitted to the Competition Policy Review Panel on the topic Canada's Foreign Investment Policy – *the Investment Canada Act,* I made the following recommendation —

"Foreign takeovers of Canadian companies should be allowed if they are in Canada's national interest. The *Investment Canada Act* should be amended to change the approval criteria from net (economic) benefit to the test of whether or not the proposed transaction is in Canada's national interest. Canada's national interest criteria would be defined and articulated by the Governor—in—Council (Cabinet) through regulation, guidelines and convention, and would focus on strategically important national assets"[6].

And I offered the following rationale –

"Since its enactment in 1985, the application of the *Investment Canada Act* by Industry Canada has become a redundant 'rubber—stamp' process. Not one takeover has been rejected since Investment Canada's inception. Incorporating the 'national interest' test would align Canada with countries like the United Kingdom, Germany, Australia and Japan – all of whom review foreign takeovers in the context of the 'national interest' or 'public interest'. A review by the federal Cabinet of all major foreign acquisitions would ensure that major Canadian corporate icons that are key strategic assets would remain in the hands of Canadians and used to advance our national objectives. Limiting the review to acquisitions proposed by state—owned enterprises and/or those transactions that run counter to our national security interests is not sufficient. A broader criterion is required"[7].

In October, 2007, I had tabled a Bill in the House of Commons, Bill C—386, *An Act to amend the Investment Canada Act (foreign investments)* that –"amends the *Investment Canada Act* to provide for the review of foreign investments in Canada that could be contrary to the national interest. This enactment also provides that the Governor in Council may, by order, take any measures that the Governor in Council considers advisable to protect the national interest".

The ability of an MP to progress a private members' bill through the House of Commons is limited by his or her ranking in the draw as laid out in the Standing Orders of the House, vis—

---

6   December 2007 brief submitted by Hon. Roy Cullen, P.C., M.P., to the Competition Policy Review Panel on the topic Canada's Foreign Investment Policy – *the Investment Canada Act*, page 3

7   Ibid, page 3

Establishing List and order of precedence at beginning of session.

> **87.** *(1)(a)(i) At the beginning of the first session of a Parliament, the Clerk of the House, acting on behalf of the Speaker, shall, after notifying all Members of the time, date and place, conduct a random draw of the names of all Members of the House to establish the List for the Consideration of Private Members' Business, and, on the twentieth sitting day following the draw, the first thirty names on the List shall, subject to paragraph (c) of this Standing Order, constitute the order of precedence.*[8]

My ranking for the draw for private members' business left me, by the bad luck of the draw, at around position number 230. It would have taken me months and years to have my bill debated in the House of Commons.

My colleague in the Senate, the Honourable Céline Hervieux—Payette, P.C., was very sympathetic to my position on foreign takeovers and on June 17, 2008 she tabled Bill S—241 in the Senate. This bill is essentially the same as my Bill C—386, with some noticeable improvements. With the dissolution of parliament in October 2008, the bill died on the Order Paper and was to be tabled again in the Senate by Céline in 2009, just in time, hopefully, to coincide with the proposed sale of Nortel's wireless assets to Telefon AB LM Ericsson. In my view these assets are strategically important to Canada and should stay here - preferably under the control of a great Canadian high tech company like Research In Motion Ltd.

I had the honour to serve as Parliamentary Secretary to Finance Paul Martin for two years (1999—2001), and later as Parliamentary Secretary to Anne McLellan from 2004 until the 2006 general election, when she was Minister of Public Safety and Emergency Preparedness and Deputy Prime Minister.

People are often confused about the role and responsibilities of Parliamentary Secretaries in the Canadian federal government. Here is a very accurate description written by the Library of Parliament, Canada —

"Parliamentary Secretaries are members of the government party who are appointed by the prime minister to assist cabinet ministers with their parliamentary duties. Under the direction of their ministers, parliamentary

---

8   Standing Orders of the House of Commons, June 2009

secretaries handle routine matters in the House of Commons, engage in committee work, and assume some extra—parliamentary responsibilities.

Parliamentary Secretaries act as a link between ministers and parliamentarians. Some may be given special assignments as well. Moreover, the office can serve as a training ground for future cabinet ministers or as a way of rewarding members of the government caucus.

Although Parliamentary Secretaries may be sworn to the Queen's Privy Council for Canada – as they were under Prime Minister Paul Martin – this has not generally been the case.

Parliamentary Secretaries receive a mandate letter from the prime minister, and carry out their responsibilities as set out by their minister. Their term of office is 12 months, which may be renewed, and they are paid an additional salary of $14,600. As public office holders, they are subject to the Conflict of Interest and Post—Employment Code for Public Office Holders, in addition to being subject to the Conflict of Interest Code for Members of the House of Commons in their capacity as members of the House of Commons.

Parliamentary Secretaries have House and public duties and department—related duties.

In the House, Parliamentary Secretaries help ministers maintain contacts with senators and other members of the House of Commons. They play a liaison role within the government caucus, particularly on matters regarding private Members' business. When the minister is away from the House, Parliamentary Secretaries may also be called upon to answer policy questions during Question Period. As well, when the subject of an Opposition Day concerns the minister's department, the Parliamentary Secretary usually lines up speakers from the government side.

Under the Standing Orders, Parliamentary Secretaries may:
- *make a statement during the time devoted to "Statements by Members" (whereas ministers may not);*
- *table documents in the House on behalf of a minister;*
- *speak on behalf of a minister during adjournment proceedings;*
- *act on behalf of a minister during consideration of the main estimates of a department in Committee of the Whole; and*
- *act on behalf of a minister during debate on a motion for the production of papers.*

Because they work under the direction of a minister, however, Parliamentary Secretaries do not pose questions during Question Period and they are ineligible to introduce their own private Member's bills or motions. They may not present government bills, either.

Parliamentary Secretaries are usually named to standing committees having mandates in their area of responsibility. There, they represent the minister's views and address political issues that may arise. They share departmental information and may work with committee chairs to plan appearances of ministers and departmental officials.

With regard to department—related duties, the prime minister may assign Parliamentary Secretaries specific policy—related priorities. In addition, while overall responsibility and accountability remain with the minister, he or she may delegate specific policy development duties to a Parliamentary Secretary. As indicated above, Parliamentary Secretaries also ensure liaison between parliamentary committees and the department.

Parliamentary Secretaries may also perform extra—parliamentary duties for the minister by fulfilling speaking engagements, attending ceremonies, or meeting delegations".[9]

Parliamentary Secretaries may also sign petitions on behalf of the Minister. A petition is a document given to an MP that must be in a prescribed format and signed by a minimum of 25 residents of Canada. It must concern a subject within the authority of the Parliament of Canada, the House of Commons or the Government of Canada. If the petition received by the MP is in 'good form' it can be tabled in the House of Commons by the MP. Each day when the House of Commons is in session, fifteen minutes are devoted to the tabling of petitions. MPs can speak very briefly to the message in the petition as it is being tabled. Petitions that are tabled daily are routed via the privy council office to the relevant minister for a response. The Standing Orders of the House of Commons require the government to respond within 45 calendar days to every petition submitted to it.

I recall my first experience dealing with a Petition while serving as Parliamentary Secretary to Minister of Finance Paul Martin. The completed response to a Petition for tabling in the House of Commons came to my office for my signature on behalf of the minister. The matter was an income tax issue from a constituent in the Province of Québec in which examples were cited to make the department's point. There were no Québec examples provided for in the departmental response – in fact the

---

9   THE ROLE OF PARLIAMENTARY SECRETARIES, Michael Dewing, Library of Parliament, Political and Social Affairs Division, 27 April 2006

examples cited in the official response were from other provinces. In my view this was inappropriate and insensitive so I asked my staff to send it back to the department for further work. A few days later I was told by my apprehensive assistant Linda Kristal that the department had advised her that they always did it this way and that no Québec examples were needed! I replied to her that if they were seeking someone else's sign off and signature, then the document could remain as it was. However, if they were looking for my signature, the Québec example would need to be there. Needless—to—say, the document was re—worked to my satisfaction and I wondered if the powerful Department of Finance was 'trying me on' and if this stand—off had helped to establish a respectful relationship with Finance Canada that I still have with this department to this day.

One of the major responsibilities of parliamentary secretaries is to work with caucus colleagues and coordinate the government's response to private members' bills and motions. Generally speaking, during my time in Ottawa, Liberal caucus members were free to vote as they wished on private member's bills and motions. That the government of the day typically had views on private member's bills goes without saying; however, depending on the impact of the bill and the associated politics, efforts to encourage colleagues to vote a certain way on such bills were handled with sensitivity and caution. The primary focus is on initiatives originating from opposition MPs, but occasionally private member's business sponsored by government MPs can create a stir as well.

Some private member's bills are far—reaching and potentially problematic for governments who are charged with the responsibility to provide responsible stewardship of the national government and parliament for the benefit of all Canadians. House of Commons rules and traditions stipulate that a private member's bill is not able to cause an expenditure of federal funds, unless the bill has the confidence of the government; i.e. unless the government supports the expenditure and indicates same to the Speaker. Interestingly, however, private member's bills that reduce federal government revenues are not ultra vires. These are the bills that often cause headaches for the government of the day.

I always considered the daily Question Period in the House to be more theatrics than substantive, but nonetheless it does provide the opposition parties with an opportunity to hold the government to account – and to score some political points!

Preparing for Question Period (QP) when the minister was not available took me first to the minister's office for a briefing by ministerial staff and someone from the department. The briefing book, or in some cases now the minister's hand held computer data base, is updated daily to reflect current issues raised by the media and the release of newly published reports. The objective is to try and anticipate what the questions might be on a given day, and discuss possible responses – recognizing that questions and answers during QP are limited to 35 seconds each – a rule that is quite strictly enforced by the speaker. Following this 15—20 minute session, it is off to meet with the house leader, his staff, and representatives from the prime minister's office to participate in a mock QP, or 'tactics' session at which time possible questions are thrown at you and your response timed and critiqued.

At 2:15 p.m. on most days, QP begins in the Chamber under the glare of the media lights and scrutiny of TV cameras. Unlike some other parliaments, such as the UK House of Commons, questions to be asked are not known beforehand and whereas the first few questions are taken by the prime minister, ministers and their parliamentary secretaries are expected to respond to questions related to their respected portfolios. QP is very boisterous and somewhat of a free—for—all and, on the government side, the goal is to stay out of trouble and stick largely to generalities. My esteemed colleague and friend, the Rt. Hon. Herb Grey, P.C., was the acknowledged master of QP when he invariably stood up in his place and told those assembled in no—uncertain terms that he did not agree with the premise of the question. Another friend and colleague, Hon. Lawrence MacAulay, P.C., when 'under the gun', would be steadfast in replying to a questioner along these lines–

"I am aware of the issue and have asked the Department to investigate the matter and report to me. Once the report is completed, the Department will send the report to me, I will then read it, and at that point in time, and not before, I will be well positioned to respond to the Member's question."

Substituting for the Minister for QP was the most intimidating thing I have ever done because you are under such scrutiny and the opposition parties are interested in one thing only – tripping you up and forcing a politically embarrassing error. However, with practice, and with the build—up of experience, the task became more manageable and the comfort index rose to a reasonable level.

It was my good fortune to have served as parliamentary secretary to two great ministers. Working with Paul Martin, my main mission was to facilitate passage of finance bills in the House of Commons and the Senate. Finance bills make up a large part of the workload in Canada's parliament– approximately 30%—35% of the legislation that finds its way into the

House of Commons emanates from the Minister of Finance. Most Finance Ministers, Paul Martin included, do not spend large amounts of time in the House of Commons debating their bills – they have other responsibilities that require their attention–so this duty rests in large part with the parliamentary secretary. On certain bills, not only did I debate the bills in the Chamber of the House of Commons, but I also appeared at the House of Commons Standing Committee on Finance, and at Senate Committee hearings, to present finance bills and take questions from MPs and Senators.

Two major pieces of legislation came forward during my tenure which we successfully steered through the various parliamentary stages to become law. The first was a restructuring of the financial services sector in this country at a time when bank mergers were very topical—resulting in major changes to the *Bank Act*. The second was the passage of the *Proceeds of Crime (Money Laundering) and Terrorist Financing Act* to fight money laundering, and the launching of Canada's financial intelligence unit – the Financial Transactions and Reports Analysis Centre of Canada (FINTRAC).

Whenever possible, I would attend weekly meetings (called CMO's then–an acronym from the time of Cohen, Mickey[10] and others) when an agenda brought various officials from Finance Canada together to meet with the Minister of Finance, the parliamentary secretary and the minister's political advisors. Often these meetings went for 3—4 hours, and sometimes the entire day (or weekend!). A host of issues would be discussed at these sessions, including preparations for the upcoming budget and economic and fiscal update. These meetings were fascinating and were very useful in building knowledge and insights into the fiscal position of the federal government and the state of the economy. It was also a great opportunity to contribute to the budget building process, and to the development of policy.

With Anne McLellan, the legislative work load was not as consuming as it was in Finance; however, national security had entered centre stage post 9/11 and as Minister of Public Safety and Emergency Preparedness, this occupied an important space for Anne and for me. Anne also delegated certain projects or files to me to lead. One such initiative was reforming the department's approach to user fees and cost recovery. User fees charged by the department covered a broad range but the biggest by far were fees charged for customs services at our borders. Given my legislative experience with user fees, the minister asked me to lead

---

10   Marshall (Mickey) Cohen was the federal Deputy Minister of Finance in the 1980's.

the development of proposals in this area to remove various inequities and change a number of anachronistic policies and procedures. Given Anne's responsibilities as Deputy Prime Minister, I was also involved in the residential schools issue – an initiative to compensate aboriginal Canadians for their historical mistreatment in federal government/church run residential schools. Another such project was the search for viable economic models for Goose Bay, Labrador, following the demise of the CFB Wing 5 base.

The Canadian Firearms Program (gun registry) fell within the jurisdiction of the Minister of Public Safety and Emergency Preparedness and one my biggest challenges was to steer the budgetary estimates for this program through parliament. No one was happy with how much it cost to develop the gun registry, but police officers were telling us that it was a useful tool for them. Not everyone, however, agreed that the gun registry was a useful or effective program – especially Canadians living in rural Canada–and this matter evoked strong emotional responses! My staff had to refer some e—mails to me on this topic to the RCMP. Working with officials in the department, we developed a PowerPoint™ presentation and began the process of meeting with key MPs in an attempt to outline the merits of the gun registry and to seek their support in committee and in the house for the budget of the Canadian Firearms Centre (CFC). This was a tough sell in some quarters but generally colleagues would listen carefully and I believe some of them were surprised with some of the positive statistics. In the end the budgetary estimates passed, to the relief of my Liberal colleagues and the management and staff at the CFC, and as a result of broad support from Liberal, Bloc, NDP, and a sprinkling of Conservative MPs.

The level of security that accompanies senior U.S. officials was made abundantly clear to me when in October 2004 The U.S. Attorney General at the time, John Ashcroft, and the head of the U.S. Drug Enforcement Administration (U.S.D.E.A.), Karen Tandy, paid a visit to Canada to participate in the Canada—USA Cross Border Crime Forum Conference. At the time of their arrival, Anne McLellan was tied up in a cabinet meeting so she asked me if I would go out to the airport to welcome them. One can imagine the level of security attached to two such high profile Americans – both committed to fighting crime, drugs and terrorism. When I arrived at the government hanger, there were RCMP and FBI agents everywhere. When word arrived that the black Gulfstream corporate jet was approaching, I was ushered out to the tarmac and stood on the carpet to await them. Interestingly, during the prior briefing I was told that the US Attorney General is the only member of the US Cabinet who is not protected by the Secret Service. He or she is provided security by the F.B.I., an agency that falls within the purview of the Attorney General. The Gulfstream jet was actually one from the FBI fleet.

When the aircraft came to a full stop, after a long pause, two larger gentlemen in suits exited down the ramp, and proceeded to walk around the aircraft and check things out. A while later, one of them exited again with a small packet which he presented to the RCMP officer dressed in full red serge who was standing next to me. After the security officer returned to the plane, my curiosity got the better of me and I asked the RCMP officer what was in the bag. Guns, was his reply. With no time to delve into the matter further, I assumed that once the US representatives arrived on Canadian soil, their security was then the responsibility of the RCMP. It was never clear to me, however, how the RCMP established whether or not all handguns had been handed over, or what all the FBI agents were doing at the airport! Was the handoff of the guns more symbolic than real, I wondered?

As Mr. Ashcroft and Ms. Tandy came down the ramp, I greeted them and welcomed them to Canada. For security reasons they split up and travelled to downtown Ottawa in separate escorted convoys where we ushered them into a waiting reception. On the way in I discovered, after trying to wind down the windows in the car I was traveling in, that they were bullet—proof and would not open.

Parliamentary secretaries are often asked to participate in various functions on behalf of the minister or in place of the minister. One of the more memorable occasions was when I was asked by the then Commissioner of the RCMP, Giuliano Zaccardelli, to officiate at the graduation ceremonies of a new batch of RCMP cadets from the RCMP Academy, Depot Division in Regina, Saskatchewan in the summer of 2005. This invitation came long before Mr. Zaccardelli created the serious problem for our Liberal Party when, in the middle of the January 2006 election campaign, he announced that there would be a probe of the Minister of Finance in connection with his handling of the introduction of a federal tax change for income trusts. The announcement came in the form of a letter from Zaccardelli to New Democratic Party Member of Parliament Judy Wasylycia—Leis.

My wife, Ethne, accompanied me to Saskatchewan for the graduation ceremony. After reporting to the office, we were escorted to a charming officers' residence just off the parade square (well within ear shot of the early morning parades!). I was honoured to be asked to inspect the cadets in a formal ceremony on the parade square. The visit also included a guided tour of the training academy, lunch with a group of cadets, witnessing the swearing—in of the cadets, and attendance at the celebratory dinner with the cadets and their families and friends where I was asked to deliver a speech after dinner. To witness the enthusiasm, energy and commitment of these young RCMP cadets first hand was an incredible experience. I was so proud of the RCMP and so disappointed later when the RCMP was hit with a barrage of problems and the confidence of Canadians in this fine police force were shattered.

Reviewing the RCMP Cadets on the parade ground at the
RCMP Training Depot in Regina

I had the great honour also to attend the memorial service for the four RCMP officers who were murdered in Mayerthorpe, Alberta which was held in Edmonton on March 10, 2005 and televised nationally on the CBC. Huge numbers of police officers from Canada and the United States were in attendance. I was particularly moved when Ian Tyson (formally of Ian & Sylvia) sang the song *Four Strong Winds*. The symbolism of the choice of that song was not lost on those assembled.

Because the Canada Border Services Agency fell within the responsibility of the Minister of Public Safety and Emergency Preparedness, I became involved in a complex tariff issue important to the bicycle manufacturing industry in Canada. I have always found trade policy and tariff rules to be somewhat of an arcane world, and these two issues proved to be no exception to this notion.

When the Peoples Republic of China (PRC) was accepted into the World Trade Organization (WTO) in 2001, and become a full member in 2006, China and all WTO member countries made many undertakings. The need to reduce Canadian tariffs on bicycles manufactured in China once a market economy had been established in the PRC was one such commitment. This development was causing much anxiety for two manufacturers of bicycles in Canada – one located in the Province of Ontario, and the other in Québec. In some countries, like the United States, the determination as to whether or not a country like China has a market economy is based on an assessment of the country as a whole. In Canada, we take a different approach and we make a decision on a sector—by—sector approach. In 2005, with the date for the elimination of tariffs on bicycles looming, the Canada Border Services Agency (CBSA), working closely with Finance Canada, began a review of the bicycle industry in China with the sole purpose of assessing whether or not a market economy for bicycles existed in the PRC. The CBSA concluded, after an exhaustive study, that a market economy was present in China for bicycles. Having conducted business in China when I was in the private sector, I questioned this result and asked for a full briefing. After that meeting, in advance of which I had prepared a number of probing questions, I came away convinced that the Departmental officials had done their home work and that there was no evidence to suggest that a market economy in this sector did not exist. We had no choice, much to the consternation of the two Canadian bicycle manufacturers, to eliminate the protective tariffs in 2006. Under Canadian trade law, however, there are provisions that allow for relief through appeal to the Canadian International Trade Tribunal, and the federal Cabinet, if products being imported into Canada are of such quantity that they pose a substantive threat to Canadian producers manufacturing the same or like products. Tariffs can be maintained until the industry can make the necessary structural changes to their business model. Canadian producers of bicycles availed themselves of these provisions. It seemed very clear to me at the time that these Canadian companies needed to alter their business strategy by moving away from the production of commodity and low cost bikes into more value added and specialty niches where they could be competitive.

On another occasion, duties on imported fabrics became an issue for clothing apparel manufacturers in the Toronto area and I became involved in a successful effort to extend a duty deferral program - a program that enables companies to defer or be relieved of the payment of duties.

In my years in the House of Commons I took great pains to adhere to the rules of the House, and to act with decorum and respect for the institution. One incident, however, in 2006 caused the speaker of the House to ask me to make a statement of apology in the Chamber. This incident occurred on November 21st, 2006 when we were debating *Bill C—24, the softwood lumber products export charge act* which was the legislation needed to implement the Conservative Government's softwood lumber deal with the United States.

I was opposed to the Conservative softwood lumber deal and I argued against it in caucus, in the media and in the House of Commons. As opposition critic for natural resources, I played a role in the development of our caucus position on the deal which was to vote against it.

In the House of Commons, I argued as follows—
"With respect to the deal, where was the Minister of Natural Resources in speaking out for communities? I understand that there are some communities whose members of Parliament are listening to the sawmills and the companies in their towns, and so they should. But companies go to them and say they would like the members to support a deal because the federal Conservative government is holding a gun to their heads. Federal ministers are saying to them that if they do not sign the deal, they will cut off all support to the forest industry.

What kind of coercion is that? That is called duress. No wonder some of the companies are saying that we should sign the deal. It is because they do not have any real choice. How can the forest products industry in Canada fight a countervailing duty claim by the United States without support from the federal government? It cannot be done. The industry knows it.

Our Liberal government supported the industry in the fight. We had a two—track process. We were supporting the industry in the fight through the NAFTA panels, the litigation and all that morass, and we were also looking at whether we could negotiate a deal. We never saw a deal that was worth cutting and the deal before us is no such deal either.

The agreement sets out certain aspects that are very disadvantageous for the forest products industry. It calls on the companies to drop their lawsuits. Once they drop their lawsuits, they can sign on and get their rebate. In fact, the rebates are going out as we speak, through the Canadian Export Development Corporation, at an irrevocable discount, I might add. If this deal is not followed through on, those companies will not be able to get the 20¢ that they have left on the table, the $1 billion that the Conservative government has left on the table.

However, some of the companies are doing it because they do not have much choice. The government has basically pulled the rug out from underneath the forest products industry in Canada.

The previous Liberal government proposed a package of $1.5 billion. In fact, in today's environment, that ante probably would have to be increased. It would have supported the industry. It would have supported the industry in using biomass energy to help companies reduce their energy costs. It was a package that would have helped them diversify their markets. The package would have helped them innovate. It would have helped them with some tax measures and made them more competitive with the U.S. softwood lumber producers and the U.S. forest products industry.

Where was the Minister of Natural Resources while the sawmills, pulp mills and newsprint operations in Quebec, Ontario and British Columbia were dropping like flies? Where was the Minister of Natural Resources in defending these forestry based communities? We do not hear from him. What initiatives has the minister come forward with? Nothing. This is a tragedy, because the forest industry is being devastated. It is being hurt very badly and we do not hear a peep from the Minister of Natural Resources……"[11]

I was never convinced that we should negotiate a softwood lumber deal with the Americans when every independent NAFTA panel and the World Trade Organization had ruled in our favour every time. I was also very concerned about the loss of sovereignty over Canadian federal and provincial forest policy such a deal could create. Also, if we caved in when we were winning all the technical arguments, what would that mean for possible future trade disputes in steel or beef cattle, or…..between our two countries when perhaps the case was not so administratively and legally strong?

David Emerson, the then Conservative Minister for International Trade, was proposing a softwood lumber deal when he had opposed such

---

11   House of Commons (Canada), Hansard, November 21, 2006

an agreement when he was a member of our Liberal Caucus. Emerson was elected in the B.C. riding of Vancouver—Kingsway in 2004 and re—elected on January 23rd, 2006 as a Liberal and two weeks later crossed the floor to become a Conservative cabinet minister. I was furious with Emerson for betraying the Liberal Party of Canada—and so were my caucus colleagues. Up until that point, David and I had had a very cordial relationship going back to the time when he was British Columbia's Deputy Minister of Finance and I was Assistant Deputy Minister in the BC Ministry of Forests. I followed his career to Alberta as head of the Canadian Western Bank, then back to Vancouver to run the Greater Vancouver Airport Authority, and finally his term as President and CEO of CANFOR – one of Canada's leading forest products companies. He and I would sometimes meet for coffee or exchange telephone calls. I called to congratulate him when CANFOR filed a Chapter 11[12] grievance under NAFTA claiming that the countervailing duties imposed on Canadian softwood lumber was the result of a biased and administratively unfair process in the United States.

The 'honeymoon' between David Emerson and me ended on February 6th, 2006 when he jumped ship to join the Conservatives.

On November 21st, 2006, in the House of Commons I sparred with Emerson on the merits/demerits of the softwood lumber deal he had negotiated.

This is what I said on that day in the House that caused a stir —

"….…..*In the last Parliament when the Liberal Party formed the government, there were a lot of discussions with the U.S. about a potential deal, but I would say that within our caucus the bar was set very high, extremely high, so high that the deal would have to be so good as to be almost perfect, because we were winning on the other track. What happened, I think, when our former minister of industry went over to the other side in a sort of horrible act of treason, if we want to call it that, was that he then came under the influence of the new republicanization of Canada's government. I think he was convinced by the Prime Minister. They had a little chat with President Bush in Cancun and*

---

12   Chapter 11 is the investment component of the North American Free Trade Agreement (NAFTA) which came into force in 1994. It establishes a framework of rules and disciplines that provides investors from NAFTA countries with a predictable, rules—based investment climate, as well as dispute settlement procedures which are designed to provide timely recourse to an impartial tribunal (Source: Foreign Affairs and International Trade (Canada) web site).

figured out a way to do this deal. The deal had been rejected by our Liberal caucus.......[13]

Two days later in the House of Commons I made the following apology—

"Mr. Speaker, I rise on a point of order. I would like to respond to a point of order that was raised by the Minister of Agriculture and Agri—Food on Tuesday, November 21 during debate on Bill C—24, the softwood lumber products export charge act.

I referred to the Minister of International Trade, that he had committed a treasonous act. I was referring to the time when he crossed over from the Liberal Party shortly after the last election to the Conservative Party. I realize that wording was unparliamentary and I would like to withdraw it. Hopefully it will end at that"[14].

Politics is a team sport and solidarity is required to advance political party goals. This does not mean, however, that one's own personal preferences and principles need to be sacrificed in the name of Party unity. Over the years I had differences with the Liberal Party and my caucus colleagues on a number of issues – the war in Afghanistan, the formal recognition by the state of same sex marriages, and election financing to name a few. Within caucus I argued my positions to the best of my ability and in most cases I adhered to the 'majority rules' principle once a final position was established – with some exceptions.

Under Prime Minister Chrétien, upcoming votes were often labeled as 'questions of confidence' to force party discipline even though they were often matters of lesser importance. Liberal Government members were usually requested by the party whip to support all government legislation in the House. In the British parliament they have a system that is called the three—line whip and this improvement was introduced by Paul Martin when he became Prime Minister.

Under this system, votes are categorized according to their importance to the government's mandate –

For legislation in the 1st Tier, government members are free to vote as they choose. This would cover legislation that the government would prefer to have adopted by the House, but not considered a priority.

Votes on legislation in the 2nd Tier are accompanied by a recommendation by the government that the specific legislation being voted on is a very

---

13   House of Commons (Canada) Hansard, November 21st, 2006.

14   House of Commons (Canada) Hansard, November 23rd, 2006.

important policy initiative; however, the vote is not considered a matter of confidence. Government members are free to vote as they wish without facing the prospect of dissolution of the House and a possible election. A number of votes against government legislation like this by a government backbencher might limit his or her upward mobility within the caucus, but that is the only repercussion.

And finally, 3rd Tier legislation is limited to key matters such as the Budget. Members of Parliament are expected to vote along party lines as the vote would be considered to be an expression of confidence or otherwise in the government.

Under Prime Minister Chrétien, the criteria which determined whether or not a vote in the House of Commons was one of confidence or not was not determined by the substance of the legislation or its origin; but rather whether or not the prime minister had made a public comment about whether or not an upcoming vote was a matter of confidence or not. It was not a legal or procedural question. It became a political question and a vote in the House was de facto a confidence matter if the prime minister so deems it! This had to change.

A case in point is Bill C—24, An Act to amend the *Canada Elections Act* and the *Income Tax Act* (Political Financing), which became law on June 19, 2003. The prime minister had stated publicly that this vote would be one of confidence or otherwise in the government. The reason (other than internal politics within the caucus) offered – is that there was a mention of the government's intention to introduce such legislation in the September 30, 2002 Speech from the Throne.

In that speech by Canada's Governor—General on this topic, the following was said –

"...the government will introduce legislative changes to the financing of political parties and candidates for office."

That was the only reference! This Act of Parliament is a voluminous document severely limiting donations to political parties by unions and corporations; but because there was a brief reference to the financing of political parties in the Throne Speech, voting for this detailed legislation was deemed by the prime minister to be a matter of confidence!

I strongly disagreed with this legislation and spoke out against it. Stephen LeDrew, the Liberal Party president at that time, called the legislation –"as dumb as a bag of hammers" – and he was not far off! My view was, and is, that the legislation was an overreaction to something that was perceived to be a problem but really wasn't. I was the only member of our caucus who voted against the legislation at second reading and I stayed away from the voting at the 3rd and final stage. While I understood that we should limit the amounts that corporations and unions could donate to federal political parties, to eliminate such donations completely flew in the face of good public policy. I was also worried that the new law would be particularly damaging to the Liberal Party (I was right about this!).

I used a case study to try and prove my point. The largest contributors to political parties in Canada were our chartered banks. They typically donated large amounts to all federal political parties – with the party in power receiving the largest amount. Surely they were in a position to influence government policy if that was the concern behind C—24. In 1998, however, their financial contributions were not sufficient to convince the government that bank mergers should proceed, even though the banks pushed this agenda very strenuously.

Some of my colleagues shared my views on this legislation. In fact, my colleague, Hon. Walter (Walt) Lastewka, PC, tried to convince Prime Minister Chrétien to limit corporate and union donations to a federal political party to $10,000 annually in an attempt to reach a compromise—but the PM would not budge. In the end the federal government and our Liberal Party were saddled with a poorly conceived piece of legislation – one that denied corporations and unions the legitimate right to support the political process, and a law that disproportionally hurt the Liberal Party of Canada.

The election of House of Commons Committee Chairs has similarly evolved. Previously, Prime Minister Chrétien, upon the recommendation of the house leader and party whip, decided which government members would chair Standing Committees of the House of Commons. These decisions, after the prime minister made them, were communicated by the whip to government members prior to the election of the chair at the relevant committee. Members voted along party lines and because of the majority of government members on each committee, the prime minister's selection in the vast majority of cases was confirmed at committee in a vote conducted by open ballot – a show of hands.

This all changed in 2002 when the House of Commons passed a motion that called for the votes for Committee chairs and vice—chairs to be conducted using a secret ballot. The use of a secret ballot was chosen simply to allow government members to vote the way they wished–and not according to the recommendation of the Whip. Over time, this could be reverted back to an open vote if members so wished–once the principle is established that members can vote for the candidate of their choice – not just for the prime minister's candidate.

I believe I can take some credit (or blame, depending on one's point of view) for this development as a result of a well—publicized controversy that occurred in 2002 when the House of Commons Standing Committee of Finance elected our Chair. I came close to being elected notwithstanding the fact that the prime minister had selected someone else. Certain members of the media had speculated that the prime minister's choice had more to do with my leadership loyalties and/ or gender; but I will leave others to decide what was behind the decision. At the election meeting, some of my colleagues broke rank, and the vote was a tie. I would have won if one of my colleagues who said he supported me hadn't abstained.

Following this event, some members of the committee went to the media and complained about the heavy—handed approach of our party Whip. I spoke out in caucus about the need to allow government MP's more latitude on issues such as the election of committee chairs, and I was strongly and uniformly supported.

After that, government caucus members began to play a key role in the selection of committee chairs. One's peers would recommend who should chair the various committees – including caucus committee chairs that also had been selected by the prime minister if you can imagine that!

One might ask why is caucus involved at all. Why not have free votes at committee? The reason for this is that, with the exception of the House of Commons Public Accounts Committee, the Government Operations & Estimates Committee, and the Standing Committee on Access to Information, Privacy and Ethics, government members chair all Standing Committees of the House. With caucus recommending to colleagues who should chair the various committees, the loss of chairs to the government by the splitting the votes of government members, accompanied by a planned and orchestrated effort amongst the opposition parties to elect a member of an opposition party as chair, is minimized. Maybe one day committee chairs could be elected freely and not according to party lines–but that is perhaps a debate for another day. The purely partisan nature of much of the House of Commons committee work would have to change, in my view, for such a change to be viable.

Members of Parliament work on a variety of issues not connected with their committee work or other defined areas of responsibility. To provide a flavor of these initiatives, the following is a sampling of some of the projects I took on during my 12½ years in the House of Commons –

- attracted federal program money to Etobicoke North to fight crime through the National Crime Prevention Program; and obtained funds to help young people exit gangs (*Breaking the Cycle* program);
- successfully worked with Ducks Unlimited, and the Nature Conservancy of Canada, to make it easier for farmers and others to donate marginal farmland for use as wetlands wildlife habitat; and for individuals to donate land to conservation agencies for designation as ecological reserves, without triggering large capital gains taxes;
- in an ironic and strange twist, tried without success to make it legal for Canadians to be able to enjoy General Mills' Fortified Cheerios™ and Wheaties™ in this country;
- developed, and presented to Caucus, a proposal to designate Etobicoke North as an International Financial Centre;
- in collaboration with a local City Councilor and the private sector, prepared a preliminary feasibility study to locate a Duty Free Zone in Etobicoke North;
- helped a local group of airport limousine drivers form their own cooperative and prepare a winning bid for Toronto Lester B. Pearson Airport limousine permits;
- obtained federal funding for a Telecommunications Learning Institute in Etobicoke North;
- steered changes to the Canadian *Income Tax Act* allowing automotive apprentices to deduct the cost of their tools for income tax purposes;
- obtained fourteen million dollars in federal funding for a local aerospace company from Technology Partnerships Canada for research and product development;
- fought for changes to the *Immigration and Refugee Protection Act* to combat marriages of convenience and marriage fraud;
- worked with the Woodbine Entertainment Group (Woodbine Racetrack), the federal Minister of Justice, and the RCMP on solutions to the problem of illegal internet gambling – a growing problem that is eroding the competitive position of horse racing tracks in Canada;

- developed a proposal for our party platform that would see the establishment of a cost of living index <u>for seniors</u>, to reflect the unique 'basket' of goods and services they encounter. This index would be used, amongst other things, for annual changes to Old Age Security and Guaranteed Income Supplement payments.
- sought changes to the *Income Tax Act* that would provide incentives for companies to establish Employee Share Ownership Plans (ESOPs).

There are some interventions as an MP that can be particularly gratifying. One such moment occurred when I was able to help a company in my riding, Soheil Mosun Limited, secure a performance bond which allowed them to undertake a major project in the United States. Soheil Mosun Limited is a custom architectural manufacturer that makes and installs exacting and quality items like elevator interiors, monumental staircases, and makes award trophies for major entertainment and book writing awards like the Genies, Geminis and the Scotiabank Giller Prize. The company, a major success story, was started by Soheil Mosun and his family in 1973 after leaving Iran to escape persecution as members of the Bahá'í faith. Soheil Mosun has now left the running of his business to his two sons, Darius and Cyrus.

A number of years ago, the company had entered a bid as part of a consortium for a major piece of work at General Motors' Global Headquarters, the Renaissance Center, in Detroit, Michigan. Their bid was successful and with that came the requirement for a hefty performance bond. They scoured the marketplace for such a bond without success. In relation to the company's size at that time, the bond was too large for the private sector to handle. Enter the Canadian Commercial Corporation (CCC)—a federal government crown corporation that I was introduced to by another government agency, the Export Development Canada (EDC). When I was asked to help Soheil Mosun Ltd., I was very familiar with EDC but had never had any dealings with CCC. The Canadian Commercial Corporation is mandated to promote and facilitate international trade on behalf of Canadian industry, particularly within government markets. Well, as a result of the introduction I made to Soheil Mosun Ltd. to the CCC, and because of the company's excellent management team and reputation for delivering quality products on time and on budget, the company was able to secure the performance bond they needed and successfully complete the project. This assignment helped the company establish a presence and reputation for quality within the US market and helped them grow their business internationally. I was very proud to have been of some assistance. Later I was able to help the company with another major project – producing and installing over 200 solid bronze windows for the restoration of the Library of Parliament in Ottawa.

Another such initiative, not as successful, involved an effort to make changes to Canada's *Income Tax Act*. A business colleague of mine in the early 1990's, fellow C.A., and Employee Share Ownership Plan (ESOP) 'guru', Perry Phillips, convinced me that we needed more employee share ownership in Canada. The statistics were staggeringly impressive showing that companies that had employees as key shareholders were more productive and more profitable. When I took the business case for enhancing ESOP tax measures to then Minister of Finance Paul Martin he told me that he did not need any convincing about the power of employee share ownership (perhaps as a result of his positive experience with Canada Steamship Lines). The problem was that at that time the Minister and the Department of Finance, with good justification, were seeking broad tax relief for Canadians and they were trying to avoid tax measures benefiting a more limited group. I tried to convince the Minister and his officials of the macro—economic benefits of enhancing Canada's economic productivity by giving workers more of a stake in profitability, but I was not able to move this item forward. Perry and I were able, however, to put the power of employee share ownership on the public policy radar. Maybe one day the changes that are required to encourage this type of behavior will be enacted. I hope so.

This is the reality of serving as an MP in Ottawa. Your success rate with initiatives that you have a personal interest in advancing can be quite variable – and somewhat disappointing at times.

A more positive result involved securing $750,000 over three years for a Telecommunications Learning Institute in Etobicoke North, and it required the dogged pursuit of the Minister of Human Resources Development. To get results I had to push hard and never let up. I finally corralled the minister in the House lobby and basically insisted that our federal government match the $3 million the Ontario Provincial Government, and the $20 million that the telecommunications industry were investing in this initiative. The project arose because the supply of telecommunications workers was not keeping pace with the rapid growth of the industry in Canada.

In every walk of life there are also some sad moments when colleagues die and time is taken to celebrate their lives and honour their passing. I recall, during my time in the House of Commons, four such emotionally changed moments in relation to former MPs Lawrence O'Brien, Shaughnessy Cohen, Charles Caccia, and Benoît Sauvageau; and former Prime Minister Pierre Elliot Trudeau.

Lawrence O'Brien was elected at the same time as I was in the 1996 set of six by—elections across Canada. He was the Member of Parliament for Labrador and replaced the very capable and affable Bill Rompkey when Bill was named to the Senate. Lawrence and I became soul mates of sorts and we sat next to each other in the Chamber of the House of Commons. For many years I traveled to Labrador with friends to fly fish in Labrador and I would often meet up with Lawrence in Goose Bay. He was a passionate and committed parliamentarian who fought tenaciously for his constituents on a range of issues – in particular making sure that Labrador got its fair share of fishing quotas. He also worked with great energy to locate businesses and jobs to Labrador as the Canadian Forces Base Goose Bay (5 Wing) was being significantly reduced in size. Lawrence can also take much of the credit for the 2003 constitutional amendment which officially changed the name of the province of Newfoundland to "Newfoundland and Labrador." As Lawrence's seat mate in the House of Commons I witnessed the gradual deterioration of his health and the courage he showed in fighting his illness. Unfortunately Lawrence succumbed to the cancer that had plagued him and he died in 2004.

When a colleague dies while serving as a sitting MP, the House of Commons will often charter a plane so that MPs can attend the funeral when it is more cost effective and efficient to do so. My day began driving to Hamilton to board, with colleagues, a Boeing 727 aircraft that then proceeded to Ottawa and then Halifax to collect more MPs and finally to Goose Bay, Labrador for the funeral. After the funeral, which attracted an overflow crowd, our attendance at the reception in the church hall was interrupted by the flight crew who strongly recommended we depart Goose Bay to escape a snow storm that was underway. We paid our respects to Lawrence's family, in particular to his devoted wife Alice, and off we went to Halifax, Ottawa – finally arriving back in Hamilton in the late evening of the same day. It had been an exhausting experience, but an occasion I wouldn't have missed. Lawrence will be remembered by those of us who knew him.

Shaughnessy Cohen represented the riding of Windsor—St. Clair for our party from 1993 until her death in 1998. On December 9, 1998, she collapsed in the House of Commons just seconds after standing to address the House. She had suffered a cerebral hemorrhage, and was pronounced dead soon afterward, despite efforts by colleagues in the Chamber like Carolyn Bennett who is a medical doctor. Shaughnessy was a bright, energetic and larger—than—life personality. A Department of National Defense Airbus transported a large number of MPs and Senators to her funeral in Windsor, Ontario where Paul Martin delivered a moving eulogy for his good friend.

Charles Caccia represented the Toronto riding of Davenport for an astounding thirty-seven years, from 1968 and 2004. I always admired Charles' passion, eloquence and integrity. Although we didn't always agree on matters of public policy, I respected him and very much enjoyed our times together. He died in 2008.

Benoît Sauvageau served as a Bloc Québécois member of the House of Commons from 1993 until his death in 2006. Although I didn't know Benoît well, he was part of a parliamentary delegation that I led to London, UK and he struck me as a very cheerful individual and someone not particularly mired in the ideology of Québec separation. Tragically, he died in a car accident in his riding of Repentigny on August 28, 2006, while on the way to a constituency event.

Finally, my wife Ethne and I had the privilege of attending the October 3, 2000 state funeral, at the Notre—Dame Basilica in Montreal, of a former Prime Minister of Canada, and Liberal Party icon, Pierre Elliott Trudeau who died on September 28, 2000. We witnessed firsthand the moving and eloquent eulogy delivered by his son, Justin Trudeau. About three thousand people gathered at the Basilica for the service, including distinguished foreign officials like Prince Andrew, Cuban president Fidel Castro, former U.S. president Jimmy Carter and the Aga Khan. All in all, it was a very moving experience.

Committees, committees, committees

When Canadians see their MPs in action it is often on the television screen during the daily Question Period which runs for forty—five raucous and theatrical minutes. This is the opportunity for the opposition parties to hold the government to account and, in a partisan way, try to demonstrate to Canadians that the government is incompetent and should be replaced. Emotions run high during QP and behavior sometimes borders on the juvenile. The reality is that Question Period is but a small part of what MPs do in Ottawa. Most of the time is spent working in committee – Standing Committees of the House of Commons, Special Committees, Joint Committees with the Senate, Caucus Committees – to name a few.

Those who watch the daily televised debates in the House of Commons on the Cable Public Affairs Channel (CPAC) are often surprised by the low turnout by MPs for the cut and thrust of debate in the Chamber. This is largely explained by the fact that Committees of the House of Commons are simultaneously in operation at this time and they overlap the debates on bills in the Chamber. By the same token, not all bills being debated in the house are of special interest to each and every MP. Watching briefs on certain bills can be accomplished by reviewing the daily Hansard – the verbatim summary of the previous day's debates; or by having a staff member follow the debate; or to consult with your caucus colleague who is the official critic on the topic.

The House of Commons is adjourned on Wednesday mornings to allow all the political parties to meet as a caucus to discuss political strategies, to decide on tactical moves in the House, and to debate internally the important public policy issues of the day and bills before the House. When

I served in the House of Commons in Ottawa, our Liberal Party Caucus consisted of all sitting Liberal MPs and Senators and comprised –

- national caucus (all MPs and Senators);
- regional Caucuses (e.g. Ontario, Québec, Atlantic Canada, Western & Northern caucus); and,
- thematic caucuses (Womens' issues, economic policy, social policy, justice, etc.)

When I first arrived in Ottawa in 1996 as a rookie MP, I was not prepared for the intensity of the debates within caucus, nor the grueling hours that MPs kept – notwithstanding my previous 'workaholic' management experience. My first caucus experience was a very heated and animated debate on same sex marriage. At that time I believe we were discussing same sex benefits, which I supported, but some in caucus viewed this measure as the 'thin edge of the wedge' towards a full recognition by the state of same sex marriage. They were right.

Depending on the size of the caucus, regional caucuses may be broken down into smaller groups. For example, in 1998, I chaired the Ontario Liberal Caucus which consisted of some 130 members of Liberal MPs and Senators from Ontario. We established sub—groups, including a Greater Toronto Area (GTA) Caucus, a Northern Ontario Caucus, an Eastern Ontario Caucus, etc. These sub regional caucuses would be the first to meet at 8 a.m. on Wednesday morning or after the House recessed on Tuesday evening. The GTA Caucus, for example, would report in at the Ontario Caucus meeting and then the Chair of the Ontario Caucus would report conclusions and recommendations at the start of the national caucus meeting at 10 a.m. on Wednesday morning. Caucus meetings, apart from reports from sub—chairs and special presentations from time—to—time from various groups, are run without agendas. These sessions provide opportunities for MPs to express their views on a variety of topics and, in the case of national caucus, speak directly to the prime minister or leader of the official opposition.

As Chair of the Ontario caucus, I became embroiled in a variety of issues - especially given the fact that this caucus comprised over one-third of the national caucus at that time, and many national issues became challenges for Canada's largest province. This was a politically important group of people representing the Liberal Party of Canada in our parliament, and we made every effort to have our voices heard. One initiative that I supported and worked hard to realize for Ontario and Canada was the ITER Canada project. Scientists from all over the world have come together in ITER (International) to work towards harnessing the energy produced by the fusion of atoms to help meet the world's future energy needs. ITER is a large-scale scientific experiment intended to prove the viability of fusion as an energy source, and to collect the data necessary for the design and subsequent operation of the first electricity-producing fusion power plant. I was attracted to this project, as were my colleagues, for a variety of reasons. Although the successful commercialization of electricity production from fusion presents daunting challenges, the payoffs are considerable. Fusion produces no carbon emissions or air pollution. It is safe, and offers a source of unlimited fuel. Besides, the construction of the plant in Ontario would provide some 30,000 construction person-years over a number of years, and the opportunity to be on the ground floor of this leading edge technology.

The ITER Agreement originally included Canada, but now is made up of China, the European Union, India, Japan, Korea, Russia and the United States.

In southern France, ITER construction is currently underway. ITER Canada was formed with the idea of attracting this project, and all of the construction and ongoing research positions, at a site in Ontario, next to the Darlington nuclear plant on Lake Ontario. The Darlington nuclear generating station produces the volumes of tritium needed for a fusion plant and would have been an ideal location. Tritium is an important fuel for controlled nuclear fusion. Canada ultimately pulled out of ITER due to a lack of funding from the federal government and withdrew from its bid for the ITER site in 2003 - but not without a fight.

In 1998, ITER Canada was very much alive and kicking. In fact, in that year ITER Canada was desperately seeking $1 million in federal funding to keep Canadian participation in the project alive. Our caucus executive, and the entire Ontario caucus, examined the business case from a federal government perspective, and decided that this was an initiative worth fighting for. I reviewed the matter with the then Minister of Natural Resources, Ralph Goodale, without success. I reported our keen interest to Prime Minister Chrétien at our national caucus meetings, and then wrote a letter to him, on behalf of the Ontario caucus, asking for $1 million in financial support. Some time elapsed without an answer, so I decided to seek a meeting with the Prime Minister's trusted Chief of Staff, Jean

Pelletier. I had never spoken to the man but he quickly agreed to meet at the PMO. At our meeting I began by speaking about the benefits of the project to Ontario and to Canada, and the need for funding so that our scientists could continue their work in Canada and abroad. Mr. Pelletier had been well briefed by officials in the Privy Council Office and he expressed concerns that the Americans and the Russians had pulled out of the project. I told Mr. Pelletier that this was not the case - the Americans and Russians were still engaged.

" Can you send me the information that you have that confirms the continued participation of the Americans and Russians in the project", he asked.

"I will have it on your desk by 7:30 am tomorrow morning", I replied.

Mr. Pelletier continued, "I have reviewed the request by the Ontario caucus with the Prime Minister, and Mr. Chrétien tells me he is not yet ready to make a decision on this matter", he asserted.

I was frustrated and annoyed with this state of affairs, and indicated same. " Mr. Pelletier, with respect, if that is where we are at, I will interpret this as a negative decision by the Prime Minister. We have scientists who have run out of money and they need to know, and as elected officials we need to know, whether or not the federal government is committed to this initiative. Without the $1 million, Canada's participation In ITER is dead", I commented.

Mr. Pelletier paused. "Mr. Cullen", he said, " in Québec we have an expression that goes like this - 's_ _t' or get off the pot. Is that what you are saying", he asked rhetorically.

"Mr. Pelletier", I responded, "in Ontario we use the same expression and it has the exact same meaning!"

"I will speak with the Prime Minister again tomorrow about this matter, and I will do my utmost to ensure that you have a decision this week", Mr. Pelletier commented. After a few pleasantries, the meeting ended.

I made sure that the information I had promised about the Russian and American participation in ITER was faxed to the Chief of Staff later that day so that he had it available for his meeting with the PM.

The week passed without a call from Mr. Pelletier. At the end of the week, on Friday evening, at my home in Toronto around 7 pm, the Prime Minister's switchboard called and asked me if I could take a call from Mr. Pelletier.

"Mr. Cullen", he said, I have some good news for you. The Prime Minister has authorized $1 million for the ITER Canada project."

Both the Prime Minister and Mr. Pelletier had come through for us. We were all thrilled.

I gained much respect for Mr. Pelletier that day. I was impressed with his wisdom, maturity, honesty and integrity. Likewise, Ed Goldenberg, senior political advisor to Prime Minister Jean Chrétien at that time, was a solid and respected advisor. Mature and seasoned individuals like Jean Pelletier and Eddie Goldenberg are worth their weight in gold - and a key ingredient for an effective and fully functional first minister's office.

Canada ultimately backed away from the ITER project, but we successfully fought to keep the dream alive for a number of years. Fusion could ultimately be the answer to our energy and environmental dilemma.

One of the most distressing aspects of the meetings of the national caucus is leaks to the press. In fact at one Caucus meeting when we were debating the war in Afghanistan and Canada's role in that conflict, someone in our Caucus reported, and misinterpreted, what I said to our leader, Stéphane Dion, in real time using a Blackberry™ wireless device. I was ambushed by Craig Oliver of CTV as I left the meeting who recited what he had been told I had said at the meeting. I was flabbergasted and very angry to think that I had been betrayed by a Liberal colleague. After all, caucus meetings are the place where MPs and Senators can speak candidly about any topic –confidentiality should be assured.

I recall being invited to a sumptuous lunch in an expensive Ottawa restaurant by a prominent national media personality. I accepted the invitation thinking that this was a 'get to know you' moment, and I was flattered by her interest. A few weeks later I became aware of the real reason for the hospitality. I received a telephone call from this reporter on a Wednesday around noon as I munched on a sandwich at my desk in my hill office. I was asked to confirm what she had heard had been discussed in our national caucus meeting that morning on a specific topic. I told her I didn't discuss what went on in Caucus. That was the last I ever heard from her!

Our national caucus on occasion, on the advice of the prime minister (or official opposition leader) and the national caucus executive, forms task groups to study various issues and report back to caucus. These task forces typically involve traveling across the country to consult with Canadians, conducting research and finally drafting a report and presenting the final product at a caucus meeting. Over the years I participated in or led various such initiatives on the following topics –

- small business enterprise —(*Clearing The Path*);
- gasoline pricing in Canada;
- future of the financial services sector (*A Balance of Interests*);
- commercializing federal government science research;
- corporate governance; and,
- Canada/USA relations.

The more cynical individuals in caucus view these task forces as a way of keeping MPs busy and feeling important, but I always learned from these experiences and witnessed some results from the fruits of our labour in the form of new policy development.

One report that had a big impact was the *Report of the Liberal Committee on Gasoline Pricing in Canada,* chaired by my caucus colleague Dan McTeague. As vice chair of the committee I worked with Dan and other colleagues as we travelled across Canada, met with 'experts' and hosted town hall meetings where ordinary citizens provided us with their views on this matter —some very animated and emotional! This process established a platform for Dan McTeague as a 'go—to' person for the media when prices escalate at the pumps. Dan is now sought out by many, and he has become very knowledgeable on this topic. He speaks for all Canadians when they witness a disconnect between world oil prices and prices at the pumps, and when prices rise dramatically just before long weekends. Our committee made a number of recommendations, some of which were implemented by our government – in particular the requirement that for predatory pricing and price discrimination, the burden of proof required in the *Competition Act* be changed to a civil rather than a criminal level of proof.

Another caucus report that the then Minister of Finance, Paul Martin, paid attention to was the *National Liberal Caucus Task Force on the Future of the Financial Services Sector* which was completed in 1998 largely as a result of the political pressure by Canada's large chartered banks on the need to merge to be more competitive. Many of us were very proud of our financial institutions in Canada and wanted to see them to grow and prosper, but we were concerned that the consolidation of our already relatively small banking sector in Canada would offer little to financial services consumers in Canada. In fact we were worried that consumers would be negatively impacted if the big chartered banks in Canada were allowed to merge. As an active member of the task force we consulted with Canadian consumers of financial services and other key stakeholders and submitted our report to the full caucus in November 1998. I was asked to write the chapter on *Competition, Competition Policy and Competition Bureau Guidelines*, which I did with enthusiasm. Our government, based on this report and others, decided not to allow bank mergers to proceed at that time but with upcoming changes to the *Bank Act* we made serious attempts to open up more competition in the financial services sector by reducing barriers to entry and encouraging the cooperative banking movement and foreign banks to compete at the retail level. Once consumers are able to access a more varied and extensive array of financial services products, I am sure Canada's chartered banks will try to make the bank merger case again. Alternatively, Canada's bankers may continue their current focus on cross border mergers and acquisitions, sensing that the mood in Ottawa for more bank consolidation may not be in the cards.

Unlike caucus committees, Standing Committees of the House of Commons are officially sanctioned by parliament and typically meet twice a week when the House is in session. Most MPs are full members of two such committees. All bills tabled in the House of Commons and passing second reading are referred to the relevant Standing Committee of the House for review, amendment and approval. Bills referred to Standing Committees almost always result in the calling of witnesses to present their views on the proposed legislation. These witnesses offer their advice on the necessity of the bill, the appropriateness of the bill as tabled in the House, and any amendments to the bill that they would propose. Depending on the complexity of the bill, and the interest in it, witnesses could be called for one or two meetings of the Committee, or as many as twenty or thirty meetings. Witnesses are typically formed into panels of four or five on any given session of the committee. They are given about ten minutes to make a presentation to the committee based on their written brief that would be available to Committee members, in both official languages, in advance of the meeting. Sometimes glitches occur when briefs are not received on time by Committee members; and/ or the brief is in English or French only. If the brief is available in one language only, it will usually be the French version that is missing – a fact that rightly does not go unnoticed by Francophone Committee members – especially those from the Bloc Québécois. From time—to—time, the Committee will refuse to deal with the witness until the brief is available in French and English. This stance is completely in accordance with Committee rules.

During the Committee meetings, simultaneous translation is available for all committee members, witnesses, clerks, research officers, media etc. to listen to the presentations and to the questions which follow from MPs.

The question period following the witness presentations allows MPs the opportunity to probe what presenters have said; assert their agreement or disagreement with some or all of the points made; clarify any ambiguities, etc. The questions typically go in rounds allocated to the various political parties, with questions and answers on the first round of questions, starting with the official opposition party and limited to seven or ten minutes each. Once all parties have had their opportunity on the first round, the second round begins and usually the time allotted is reduced to perhaps five minutes. The allocation of the time for questions is decided by the committee at the beginning of a session and it requires a good chair to keep the meeting moving in an orderly, fair and disciplined manner.

Interested parties may not wish to appear in front of the committee but submit a brief with their views on a bill. When they do this, their brief, in the committee member's language of choice, is circulated to all committee members by the committee clerk.

Following the consultation period, the committee will review a summary prepared by the committee research staff of the points expressed and any amendments proposed. This approach would typically be followed with more complex legislation; otherwise, the committee will proceed soon afterwards to clause—by—clause consideration of the Bill. The Bill proponents (often government departmental officials) are typically there as witnesses to respond to any questions the Committee members may have about specific provisions of the bill, and the implications of proceeding with any proposed amendments. The departmental officials are supported by the portfolio minister's parliamentary secretary who is a member of the committee and there to vet any committee concerns and consider any amendments; but equally importantly to support the government in its efforts to advance the bill and report the Bill back to the House of Commons for Report Stage (2nd Reading).

Standing Committees also conduct special studies, not related to Bills in the House, from time—to—time and report their results with recommendations to Parliament and the government of the day. I have participated in many such studies, some of the more memorable being –

- *A National Highway Renewal Strategy* (Standing Committee on Transport 1997);
- *The Renaissance of Passenger Rail in Canada* (Standing Committee on Transport 1998)
- *Challenge for Change – A Study of Cost Recovery* (Standing Committee on Finance 2000);
- *Various Pre—budget Consultation Reports* (Standing Committee on Finance);
- *The Oil Sands: Toward Sustainable Development* (Standing Committee on Natural Resources 2007);
- *Rights, Limits, Security: A Comprehensive Review of the Anti— Terrorism Act and Related Issues* (Standing Committee on Public Safety and National Security 2007);
- *Counterfeit Goods in Canada – A Threat to Public Safety* (Standing Committee on Public Safety and National Security 2007);
- *Review of the Witness Protection Program* (Standing Committee on Public Safety and National Security 2008); and,
- *Study of the Conductive Energy Weapon—Taser®* (Standing Committee on Public Safety and National Security 2008).

Work on Standing Committees can be very different depending on whether or not one is one the government side or in opposition, or whether the government is a majority or minority government. A few cases follow to illustrate this contrast.

While serving as parliamentary secretary from 1999 to 2001 to the then Minister of Finance, Paul Martin, we were a majority government under the leadership of Prime Minister Jean Chrétien. As parliamentary secretary, my mission in the House of Commons and the Senate was to expedite the passage of Finance bills. Bills emanating from the Minister of Finance and Finance Canada, rightly or wrongly, take on a special aura because often these bills are matters of confidence. After a bill reached the House of Commons Standing Committee on Finance, it was not a huge challenge in a majority parliament to obtain the support of my Liberal colleagues on the committee to pass the bill without amendment and report it back unchanged to the House. Given this environment, I tried to give opposition members on the committee the chance to bring forward amendments – my only requirement being that I would need to see the amendments at least two days before the bill went into clause—by—clause consideration (i.e. when the bill was to be finally voted on at committee). I promised that if that lead time was provided, I would review the proposed amendment with the Department of Finance, and the Minister if necessary, and either accept the amendment or provide an explanation of why we would oppose it. Regrettably, most or all amendments were tabled too late for this type of review. Often, amendments are tabled for crass political reasons, with no real intent to seek their passage.

There are occasions when government MPs in a majority government balk at supporting government bills, or defeating a popular private members' bill. There are many cases in point. There are four instances that I particularly recall when I was personally involved.

Following my term as chair of the House of Commons Standing Committee on Finance and as parliamentary secretary to the minister of finance, I sat as a regular member of the Standing Committee on Finance. I incurred the wrath of the Prime Minister's Office when I proposed an amendment to a budget implementation bill which would have increased the mineral exploration tax credit for the mining industry from 10% to 20%. I believed such a move was necessary to stimulate more exploration for metals and minerals as our reserves became increasingly depleted. I was the only Liberal MP who voted for this amendment which was ultimately defeated.

On another occasion, just prior to the 2004 general election, while serving as parliamentary secretary (PS) to the Minister of Finance, one of the many private member' bills dealing with mechanics tools was on the floor of the House of Commons and would be voted on before parliament was dissolved for the election. The bill, not unlike many other bills that had come before the House previously on this topic and been defeated, called for amendments to the *Income Tax Act* to allow mechanics to deduct the cost of their tools in the calculation of their net income. There had been provisions in the *Act* which permitted the deduction of expenses incurred to generate income, but they were very restrictive, if not non—existent, and were certainly not sufficient to cover the costs of the tools required by mechanics to perform their work. This proposed legislation was very attractive politically to most MPs in the House of Commons, especially with an election looming. Just imagine how many mechanics there are in ridings across the country, and how many votes could be garnered from them and their family and friends on polling day! As PS I had worked with the Department of Finance to analyze the Bill and assess its budgetary impact. Officials in the department were very concerned about how open ended the Bill was. They were worried that passage of this amendment would open the door for the deduction of a much wider variety of employment tools, including lap tops, blackberries, and cell phones. They wanted to 'ring fence' the provisions to limit their application and minimize the fiscal impact. The Department was much more comfortable limiting the deduction to tools for mechanics' apprentices. Not only would this 'ring fence' the fiscal cost, but there was a policy rationale to it in that apprentices faced the biggest challenge as they built up their tool inventory at the start of their career. Various amendments had failed and a vote was looming. I had spoken to my caucus colleagues and recommended against the bill – with the promise that when we were re—elected (one always thinks positive thoughts in golf and politics), our government would introduce amendments to the *Income Tax Act* to permit mechanic apprentices to deduct the cost of their tools on an amortized formula over a few years. While my colleagues understood the logic of this and the need to be fiscally prudent, they were much more skeptical about voting against such a popular piece of legislation just prior to a general election. Based on a cursory straw poll I concluded that we could win the day on this bill and defeat it in the House. How wrong I was to be!

As the vote was being tallied, it became clear that the vast majority of my Liberal colleagues, together with all opposition MPs, would be voting in favour of the Bill. The bill was going to pass, leaving many of our colleagues in the uncomfortable position of voting against a popular Bill that would pass anyway. Paul Martin made a quick decision and spread the word amongst our ranks that Liberal colleagues were free to vote as they wished. Upon dissolution in a few days, the Bill would also 'die' on the order paper and its proponent would have to begin all over again. Seated behind the Finance Minister in the Chamber, I leaned forward and asked Paul if he had any objection if I voted against the Bill – on the grounds that I would be working in the trenches when we returned to Ottawa to bring in the amendments we supported – i.e. limiting the deduction to mechanics' apprentices. I believed that if I had voted in favour of the private members' bill currently before the House, my credibility would be called into question later. The Bill passed, the vote was called, and parliament was dissolved a few days later. Following the election I worked with the department of finance and caucus colleagues and in our first budget following the 2004 election, the finance minister brought forward the 'ring fenced' amendments to the *Income Tax Act*. The budget was supported by the House of Commons, the *Budget Implementation Act* was subsequently passed, and these provisions positively impacting mechanics' apprentices are now law. The Private Members' Bill dealing with this topic made its way back into the House in due course, and it was defeated with the support of Liberal colleagues – confident that our government had brought forward similar, if not the same, legislative measures. While this process was lengthy and cumbersome, in the end I believe Canadian taxpayers benefited.

My private members' Bill C 212– *An act respecting user fees*, which ultimately was passed by both houses of parliament and received royal assent on March 31, 2004, is another example of how a backbench MP can initiate the passage of legislation in Canada—even when his own government opposes it. In fairness, our government supported the elements of greater accountability and transparency that my bill brought to the treatment of user fees, but the president of the treasury board at the time was concerned about the fiscal impact of my bill as federal departments and agencies attempted to meet the more stringent performance standards demanded by the bill.

When the bill was finally adopted by Parliament, the Clerk of the House of Commons – a real professional who had served in the House of Commons for some 25 years, told me that the bill was the most comprehensive and complicated private members bill that he had ever seen adopted by Canada's Parliament. I was very proud!

To get the bill passed, I had to 'trade—up' to a higher rank on the priority list for private members' business on a number of occasions and exchange with MPs who were not ready to proceed with their bills. This required a concerted and focused effort to achieve results. Fortunately, Dave Cuddemi, my Executive Assistant, persevered and by staying on top of this project he did some very astute bill 'swapping'.

Companies in my former riding of Etobicoke North – companies like Bayer Canada and BASF Canada – who are exposed to federal government fees for drug approvals, or approvals of chemical products, do not argue about the appropriateness of user fees for proprietary services. They understand that this is required. These companies came to visit me sometime in 1999 and argued, however, that user fees were seriously eroding their competitiveness because the fees were increasing with no corresponding increase in service or performance. The timelines for drug and chemical approvals were way out of line with countries like the USA and the United Kingdom.

My private member's bill, now an Act of the Parliament of Canada – Bill C—212, *An Act respecting user fees,* is designed to bring greater transparency and accountability to federal government departments and agencies when they attempt to recover costs through user fees.

I introduced this Bill because of a certain level of frustration with the lack of progress on this issue. The House of Commons Standing Committee on Finance in 2000 (*Challenge for Change – A Study of Cost Recovery*) recommended significant changes to the cost recovery/user fee policy, but progress by our Liberal government had been slow to non— existent.

Bill C—212 potentially affects Canadians from coast to coast to coast because it applies to federal government departments, agencies, boards, commissions or any other body, with the exception of crown corporations, that has the power to fix a user fee or a cost recovery charge under the authority of an Act of Parliament. Thus, in addition to a fee for the approval of a new drug, consumer specialty product, or chemical molecule, individuals paying fees to visit a federal park, or those passengers paying the Air Travelers Security Charge, or businesses paying a fee to access the MERX government procurement system, or individuals paying a fee to the Passport Office for a passport, or provincial or territorial authorities paying fees to the Canadian Coast Guard for ice—breaking services, would also be affected by this bill.

I have always supported the government's objective to recover costs through user fees for private goods or proprietary services. What my legislation addressed, were the following concerns:

- the need for more parliamentary oversight when user fees are introduced or changed;
- the need for greater stakeholder participation in the fee—setting process;
- the need for improved linkages between user fees, and federal department and agency performance specifications and standards;
- the requirement for more comprehensive stakeholder impact and competitiveness analysis when new user fees, or fee increases, are contemplated;

- the need for increased transparency with respect to why fees are applicable, what fees are charged, what costs are identified as recoverable, and whether performance standards are being met;
- the need for an independent dispute resolution process to address the complaints or grievances of the payers of user fees; and,
- the need for an annual report outlining all user fees in effect that would be tabled in the House of Commons, and referred to the appropriate Committee of the House (Finance).

When I introduced my bill I believed that it was time for the Parliament of Canada to take greater ownership of user fees. What began as a legitimate attempt to more fully recover costs for proprietary services had developed into something that is beyond that which was contemplated. User fees bring in $4 billion annually in revenues for the federal government. Departments and agencies of the federal government had, in many cases, expanded the concept and introduced user fees, and increased user fees, beyond what is reasonable, and, more often than not, without any reference to service or performance standards. Let us keep in mind – these are monopolies that were increasing their prices! In my view it was time to introduce more transparency and accountability into the user fee process, and this was accomplished with the passage of Bill C—212.

In a minority parliament committee work takes on different forms, and often results in a more effective voice for MPs. In 2005 the Standing Committee on Public Safety and National Security was reviewing a Liberal government Bill C—13 which proposed amendments to Canada's DNA legislation governing the National DNA Data Bank. At that time I was serving as parliamentary secretary to Hon. Anne McLellan, P.C., Minister of Public Safety and Emergency Preparedness and Deputy Prime Minister. I had raised concerns with the volume of DNA that was finding its way to the RCMP administered National DNA Data Bank with the then Minister of Justice. I was told that, at that time, only about 50% of the DNA that should have been sent to the DNA lab was being sent there. Registering the DNA of convicted criminals in the data bank helps to prevent and solve crimes. I was very concerned that, for some reason, judges and crown prosecutors were not insisting in all cases on the transfer of DNA to the Data Bank on conviction – especially for the most serious crimes.

During clause—by—clause consideration of the bill, the Conservative justice critic at the time, Hon. Vic Toews, P.C. tabled an amendment to the bill that would remove judicial discretion in the decision as to whether or not to send the DNA of a criminal convicted of serious crimes to the DNA Data Bank. I was intrigued by this amendment because it went to the heart of my concerns, and my discussions with the Justice Minister were not producing any results. The DNA Bill emanated from the Minister of Justice and his parliamentary secretary, Hon. Paul Macklin, P.C. was before the Committee at clause—by—clause consideration. When it came to my turn to ask a question of the parliamentary secretary and the Department of Justice officials who accompanied him, I asked if the officials could provide an example of when it would be in the national interest for a judge to withhold the transmission of the DNA of a criminal convicted of a serious offence to the DNA Data Bank. When they could offer no such examples, I decided that I would support the Conservative amendment. We agreed to 'stand down' the clauses of the bill connected to this amendment, vote in favour of the other clauses, and sleep on the amendment. Even the Bloc Québécois supported the Conservative amendment.

When the meeting adjourned for the day, a reporter from the Ottawa Citizen approached me and said to me that in her 10 years of covering the hill she had never witnessed two parliamentary secretaries in disagreement over a bill. My comment to her was that when it came to protecting the public and providing law enforcement authorities with the tools they needed to do their job, I was a 'bit rednecky'. She used this term in an article in the next day's edition of the Citizen which provoked a few laughs from my colleagues. Nonetheless, overnight we reached a compromise with the Conservatives on the Committee and their list of offences was pared down to the most heinous of crimes like murder and rape. The bill passed with the adjusted amendment and now judges do not have any discretion in the transmission of DNA of convicted criminals to the National Data Bank for particularly serious crimes. I was proud of the role that I and other Committee members played in producing what I believe is better DNA legislation. What we accomplished at the Committee would have been difficult, if not impossible, in a majority government.

Meetings of Standing Committees can sometimes take interesting turns. In 2007 the Standing Committee on Public Safety and National Security conducted a comprehensive review of Canada's *Anti—Terrorism Act*, including a review of the contentious instrument known as Security Certificates. Security Certificates allow the federal authorities to detain and deport foreign nationals and all other non—citizens living in Canada if they are suspected of violating human rights, or associated with organized crime, or considered a threat to national security. At that time I was parliamentary secretary to Anne McLellan, the Minister responsible for national security and for the Canadian Security Intelligence Service (CSIS). At that time there were, I believe, six or seven individuals being detained in Canada under Security Certificates. I asked officials in the Department of Public Safety if it would be possible for a representative from the department to appear as a witness at the Public Safety and National Security Committee and share a security dossier, 'whiting out' comments that would compromise our sources, with the Standing Committee. They told me they would check it out and advise me.

A few days later I was informed that a briefing book outlining the government's case against an alleged Iranian assassin could be prepared with only certain paragraphs eliminated to protect our allies and other sources. I instructed the Department to proceed in this way and notified the Clerk of the Committee of our intentions.

On the day of the Committee meeting when the dossier was presented, a panel of 4—5 witnesses rounded out the presence of the departmental official – a senior and seasoned Senior Assistant Deputy Minister – Paul Kennedy. One of the other witnesses was a representative of the British Columbia Civil Liberties Association. After the presentation by the Senior ADM in which he described the profile of the alleged Iranian assassin who was being detained on a Security Certificate, I felt that the case was very convincing and provided a solid rationale for his detention, and so I decided on a somewhat risky question to pose to the representative from the BC Civil Liberties Association. I asked him, now that he had been briefed about this individual who was being held under a Security Certificate, if he would like to have this person as a next door neighbour. I held my breath for his answer.

"No" he replied.

"If that is the case", I asked, "why does the BC Civil Liberties Association have such a problem with Security Certificates?" He responded that it was the process that they had problems with.

He did have a point about the process and our Committee made a number of recommendations to improve the transparency and fairness of the proceedings leading up to the issuance of a Security Certificate.

At the time of writing, Security Certificates look to be a thing of the past. The Conservative Government is examining alternatives that will balance the need to respect civil liberties and at the same time provide a safe and secure environment for Canadians. This is not an easy task.

During my term as Vice-Chair of the Standing Committee on Transportation, we focused much of our time and energy examining issues associated with rail transportation in Canada, and we provided Parliament and the Minister of Transportation at the time, David Collenette, with a number of recommendations. Those dealing with VIA Rail and passenger rail services generally found their way into our 1998 report entitled *The Renaissance of Passenger Rail in Canada*.

We learned at that time that VIA's service network is composed of four main groups:
- the Québec City-Windsor corridor, which accounts for nearly 85 per cent of the company's total passengers and some 70 per cent of its income;
- "western" services, which run between Toronto and Vancouver;
- "eastern" services, which link the Atlantic regions with central Canada via the Montreal-Halifax and Montreal-Gaspé routes; and "northern" services in remote and sparsely populated regions in Québec, Ontario, Saskatchewan and British Columbia.

The members of the Standing Committee viewed passenger rail as a partial solution to alleviate the congestion and environmental problems associated with our crowded highways and airways. Rail services typically leave a smaller environmental footprint when compared with road and air transportation. The consensus view of committee members was that putting passengers into trains instead of automobiles, and moving goods by train rather than truck, had great positive potential. We wanted to remove, where possible, any obstacles to achieve this objective, but a number of challenges loomed. The Standing Committee on Transportation conducted extensive hearings in Canada and traveled to the United States and France to learn of the experiences of Amtrac, and the Société Nationale des Chemins de fer Français (French National Railway Company or SNCF) respectively.

Some passenger routes, like the run between Toronto and Vancouver, and other remote services, were losing money and needed attention. In addition, VIA needed a long term commitment from the federal government for capital and operational funding to sustain its network and grow its business. The Québec City-Windsor corridor posed some unique challenges given the heavy volume of passenger and freight services along that route. VIA needed more 'slots' on these routes to allow them to be more competitive by providing customers with more travel options and more frequent departures. What we learned as part of this exercise is that passenger trains consume some 3-4 times more capacity on railway tracks than do freight trains. The reason for this is because passenger trains travel faster and more space is needed between trains for safety reasons. Because of the rail congestion in the Québec City-Windsor corridor, CN and CP were reluctant to agree to more slots for VIA. Interestingly, in the United States, by virtue of the *Rail Passenger Service Act* in that country, Amtrac trains take priority over freight trains. In other words if a freight train and an Amtrac train are competing for space on the track, it is the freight train that is obliged to pull off onto the siding. It is the complete opposite in Canada where freight trains have priority over VIA. When we subtly threatened to bring in the US approach on rail priority with like legislative changes in Canada, suddenly, but not surprisingly, CN and CP came up with more slots for VIA; but with the benefit of hindsight, not enough for VIA to be fully viable in this corridor.

To address the Québec City-Windsor corridor capacity problem, members of the committee were intrigued by a proposal for a TGV (*Train à Grande Vitesse*, meaning *high-speed train*). In 1998, the Lynx consortium, including Bombardier and SNC- Lavalin, proposed a 320 km/h high-speed train from Toronto to Quebec City via Kingston, Ottawa and Montreal based on the TGV and the French Turbo-Train technology. This project would involve a new railway bed and tracks and would take pressure off the existing infrastructure. Lynx had completed a pre-feasibility study which indicated a positive business case based on a capital cost of some $11 billion, including loan guarantees from the federal government. The proposal, albeit an expensive one, was interesting because -

- it would take pressure off the existing rail infrastructure and revitalize passenger rail in the corridor;
- moving people off the highway and out of aircraft and onto the TGV would have positive environmental benefits;
- One could travel between Toronto and Montreal, downtown to downtown, in two hours and twenty-one minutes which was competitive with air travel when one took into account travel to and from airports;
- the Lynx TGV price points were very competitive with comparable air fares;
- given the speed of the trains and safety considerations, the Lynx project consisted of only one railway crossing on the route - all

other intersections were engineered for the railway line to go over or under the highways or to by pass them altogether;

- two icon Canadian companies, Bombardier and SNC Lavalin and other companies, would position Canada strongly in the fast train market; and
- Canadian jobs and sizable economic activity would be created should this project proceed.

As an interim step, Lynx approached the federal government seeking a $33 million contribution so that they could undertake an 'investment grade' business case analysis that would cost $100 million. The other $67 million would be shared equally by the Québec and Ontario provincial governments. If this study showed that the project delivered a positive return-on-investment, then it could be financed by the private sector - accompanied by a federal loan guarantee. Although we shared the Minister's concern about the loan guarantee, we believed the federal government should show some leadership to keep the idea alive and we recommended the following -

"Given the potential for high-speed rail in the corridor, the government should participate with the governments of Québec and Ontario in Phase II of the Lynx proposal to a maximum of $25 million over 41 months, with the balance of government funds coming from the provinces of Québec and Ontario"[15].

To which the government responded -

"The Lynx proposal to build a high-speed rail network from Toronto to Québec City is very complex and requires further analysis before a decision is reached or before proceeding with any future phases"[16].

What a pity and opportunity lost. While there have been other TGV proposals that have floated around in Canada since 1998, the idea is still only a dream.

---

15   the Renaissance of Passenger Rail in Canada - Report of the Standing Committee on Transport - Raymond Bonin, Chairman, June 1998

16   http://www.tc.gc.ca/eng/mediaroom/releases-nat-1998-98_h100e-2210.htm

Rum, Rations, Pay, Perks and Pensions

The dinner party with friends starts out in the usual way and at some point in the evening ends up engaging us all in the following typical dialogue –

"So Roy, as a federal MP, how much time do you spend in Ottawa," I am asked.

"The House of Commons typically sits for 125—130 days each year, so on those days I would be in Ottawa unless I was traveling on committee business, or part of an international parliamentary delegation, or accompanying a minister on government business" I answer—believing that people are sincerely interested and much in the dark about the life of their elected officials.

More probing follows, "Do you travel back and forth to Ottawa by train, by plane or do you drive", I am asked.

"As a Toronto area MP, I find it much more convenient and productive to fly and only on rare occasions would I take the train or drive", I respond wondering if those assembled approve of such use of their tax dollars.

"Do you have an apartment in Ottawa?" a new participant continues.

"In my twelve years as a federal MP, I have tried different types of accommodation including living in a hotel, sharing an apartment with a fellow MP, and more recently renting a duplex on my own" I reply.

"Well Roy, who pays for all of this? Does the House of Commons provide you with a budget? How much did it cost you personally to run for parliament?" I am asked.

These are two very different questions and somewhat 'loaded' so I step out on the ice carefully.

"Yes, the House of Commons provides each MP with an office budget to cover the costs of running their Ottawa and constituency offices. Some

MP's, especially those from rural Canada, need more than one constituency office. As an urban MP, I have my office on the hill, one constituency office and seven full and part time staff members. My member's operating budget is $280,000 which covers the salaries for all my staff, my constituency office lease, equipment and supplies, utilities, advertising, and other expenses. There are other expense allowances for travel, accommodation in Ottawa, and telephone calls", I answer.

"Running for elected office is a different matter", I point out.

"Partisan activities are not funded by the House of Commons so the funds required to mount and run an election campaign and to engage in strictly political activities are my responsibility" I respond.

"Do you enjoy being an MP?" someone in the dinner party group asks.

"I do, but the job is not for everybody" is my usual answer.

"What motivated you to run for a seat in the House of Commons?" another seated at the table asks.

"Well, in 1996, I was fifty years of age and an opportunity presented itself to me to run, and I believed I could make a contribution to Canada in the House of Commons. I concluded that it was going to be then or never, so after consulting with my wife and others, I decided to take the plunge", I explained.

This type of dialogue, and these types of questions, convinced me that most Canadians were interested in what went on in Ottawa and what Members of Parliament do. By the same token, I was amazed how scant their information was about both the role of an MP and how decisions are made in our capital city.

In my last full year as an MP, for the fiscal period from April 1, 2007 to March 30, 2008, my expenditures paid by the House of Commons broke down as follows –

Staff and other expenses	$252,678
Travel	94,920
Office lease	16,680
Printing	14,875
Telephone	8,222
Advertising	6,173
Office supplies	5,872
Other	255
Total expenditure	$399,675

Of this $399,675 total, $276, 246, or 69% came through my Member's Office Budget (MOB), and the balance were goods and services provided directly by the House of Commons (e.g. printing, travel, telephone, and office supplies). Fully 63% of my expenses were paying staff to support me in my work in Parliament and in supporting my constituents. I believe that these resources were sufficient, and not excessive. They allowed me to perform my job.

As an MP I encouraged Canadians to visit their parliament in Ottawa and I hosted many constituents to a tour of the parliament buildings, lunch in the parliamentary restaurant with me and as my guest, into the visitors' gallery for Question Period, and often a photo with the prime minister in his office. The people who participated in this tour program always remarked how glad they were to have seen the House of Commons close—up and how educational the experience was.

Many Canadians don't have a very clear picture of what goes on in Ottawa or what MPs do. Many would be surprised by the comment made recently by the well—known and respected chief economist of the Toronto—Dominion Bank, Don Drummond, when he retired in 2010. When asked if he would consider a career in politics he was quoted as saying –
"I have had the benefit of working for politicians for 23 years and it is a lot harder work than people can imagine. I am not interested.[17]" Don worked in the federal Department of Finance for 23 years, rising to the level of associate deputy minister. I got to know Don, and respect his abilities, when I was Paul Martin's parliamentary secretary.

The ambivalent or jaundiced view that Canadians have of MPs was reinforced for me one time when two young mining industry union representatives from Sudbury came to town. After the terrible 1992 Westray Mine disaster which resulted in the deaths of 29 miners in Nova Scotia, they were lobbying for changes to legislation to increase the sanctions to officers and directors of mining companies where such incidents occurred. The union representatives called my office and asked to meet with me. At that time, I also had an interest in directors' liability issues and had tabled my first bill in the House of Commons which would allow directors of companies incorporated under the *Canada Business Corporations Act* the defense of 'due diligence'. Too many quality individuals were refusing to accept appointments to boards of directors to these companies because

---

17 National Post, March 12, 2010, page FP 3

they were worried about legal liabilities they might incur when things went wrong after the board had done all they could, asked the right questions, brought in the appropriate 'experts', etc. The change I proposed would align the *Canada Business Corporations Act* with other similar provincial laws across Canada. Soon after my bill was tabled, Industry Minister John Manley made these same changes to government legislation which were adopted by Parliament—so I dropped my bill as it was then redundant.

Now let's get back to the two Sudbury union representatives. Given my interest in the liabilities of directors, I asked my Ottawa assistant to schedule a meeting with the two individuals as soon as possible since they were staying in Ottawa for a short period of time. When they arrived at my office at the appointed time, they sat down and the conversation went somewhat as follows –

"Mr. Cullen, we can't thank you enough for taking the time to meet with us" they offered in unison.

"Have you been having difficulty arranging meetings with MPs and Senators" I enquired.

"We had no idea how busy your schedules or the demands on your time" one of them volunteered.

My curiosity piqued, I offered a theory "So, before this visit to Ottawa, was your impression one in which MPs lounged around all day, smoked cigars, and did media interviews" I asked.

"Yes, to be honest, that was exactly the image we had conjured up and boy have we ever learned a lot" they answered.

We then ventured into the more arcane world of directors' liability, but from that day forward I committed myself to bringing as many Canadians to Ottawa as possible, with some success. Each year I donated to the annual fundraiser of the Etobicoke General Hospital, and later the William Osler Health Centre, at their silent auction, a complimentary tour of the parliament buildings, lunch in the parliamentary restaurant, question period, and a photo opportunity with the prime minister. This item typically fetched in the range of $500—$700 each year and was well received.

The role of an MP is to represent his/her constituents in the House of Commons and to contribute to national public policy making. This might, in some instances involve promoting ideas and initiatives that are quite specific to your riding–a local priority. For example, Etobicoke North regrettably is plagued with criminal activity characterized by gangs, drug dealing and gun violence. For this reason I spent countless hours debating and promoting solutions on how best to respond to this type of behavior, and how we could make our streets safer. Did we need to stiffen the provisions for gun related crime in the *Criminal Code*? Were more or different types of policing required? Should handguns be banned? Did sentences and jail time for convicted criminals need to be increased? Were more efforts required at the community and family level to prevent crimes before they were committed? My vociferous opposition to handguns, and the senseless crimes they facilitated, led to a press conference in my riding during the 2006 election campaign at which time Prime Minister Paul Martin announced in person that, if re—elected, our Liberal Party would ban the possession of handguns in Canada – with very limited exceptions to this restriction. This move, which I strongly supported, was very well received in Etobicoke North, but was not so popular in other constituencies.

Likewise Lester B. Pearson Airport is close to Etobicoke North and it generates both positive economic activity and some negative environmental issues. Because of these impacts on my community, I took a great interest in airport issues and involved myself in various federal policy matters affecting the airport.

Sometimes local industrial interests in my riding would raise issues of concern to them—everything from regulatory matters, to taxation issues, to international trade disputes and the full gamut of business—related problems and opportunities. Etobicoke North is home to a large number of small, medium and large companies, employing many constituents. Their federal issues, if reasonable, became my issues especially from the perspective of employment protection and growth.

Because Etobicoke North is so ethnically diverse, immigration issues are always front and centre for the majority of the local residents. For the local MP this would involve trying to resolve visitor visa problems, speeding up sponsorship applications, de—bugging citizenship application issues, listening to and sometimes engaging in refugee claims and deportation orders, etc. There was one individual on my staff in Toronto who worked exclusively on immigration matters.

It is the responsibility of the MP to engage also on issues of national importance that are of more general interest to one's constituents and to all Canadians. My twelve and one—half years in the House of Commons drew me into a number of debates and discussions—too numerous to describe here—but it would include policies and programs related to the war in Afghanistan, same—sex marriage, federal fiscal policies, tax policies and deficit fighting strategies, *Criminal Code* amendments, employment insurance, Canada's pension system, anti—terrorism laws, and healthcare—to name but a few. On matters like these, I listened to what my constituents had to say and I married this up with advice that I received from other sources (e.g. ministers/caucus/bureaucrats/non—governmental organizations/academics) and then I would reach my own conclusion on how to vote on a particular bill–assuming that I had some latitude on a question that was not one of confidence in the government.

One quickly discovers that public policy and politics sometimes don't mix very well. The policy might be a good one, but it may not be popular; or, conversely, the policy may have broad appeal, but from a public policy perspective it is deficient. There are very few policies that appeal to everyone, except perhaps reducing taxes - but even this measure some would argue against on the grounds that important services will be negatively affected. There is no better example, in my view, in Canada of this conflict between policy and politics than that embodied in the Goods and Services Tax (GST)/ Harmonized Sales Tax (HST).

First, some philosophical context. French Minister of Finance under King Louis XIV Jean Baptiste Colbert once made the wise observation - "The art of taxation is so plucking the goose as to get the most feathers with the least hissing." In my graduate work in public administration I learned about the principle of Pareto's law (Vilfredo Pareto was an Italian sociologist and economist who lived from 1848 to 1923), to optimize results when compromises were required such that the winners of any policy change exceeded, hopefully by a wide margin, the losers. This desired state often poses some challenges.

Brian Mulroney's Conservative government introduced the GST in January 1991. The GST replaced a hidden 13.5% Manufacturers' Sales Tax (MST) which was subject to abuse, and the MST also rendered some Canadian companies uncompetitive. It was the right tax to introduce at that time. The Liberal Party argued against it recognizing that the general public didn't like it especially since most Canadians didn't realize they were paying the MST, whereas the GST would be a very visible tax. During the 1993 federal election campaign Jean Chrétien promised to replace/scrap the GST (good politics/bad policy) - another controversial step because we were never able to deliver on this promise (bad politics/good policy).

Once in government in 1993 it became evident to us some years later that it would be good policy to raise the GST and reduce personal income taxes by a comparable amount. The rationale for this was the level of various taxes in Canada compared with other OECD countries, vis -

"In 1997, Canada's overall taxation ranked in the middle of the G-7 countries and the 29 members of the Organisation for Economic Co-operation and Development (OECD). The story is mixed, however, when the various components are compared.

Canada's personal taxes were the highest of the G-7 nations and among the highest in the OECD. Its corporate taxes were in the middle of the G-7 and ninth highest of the 28 OECD countries for which data are available. Canada's payroll taxes were the lowest in the G-7 and the ninth lowest among all 29 OECD member states. Its property taxes were the second highest among both the G-7 nations and the 28 OECD member countries for which data are available. Canada's goods and services taxes (also known as consumption taxes) were the third lowest in the G-7 and among the lowest in the OECD (fifth lowest)".[18]

In summary, in 1997, the federal tax burden of Canadians looked like this -

Tax	Ranking
1. personal income taxes	Canada highest of other OECD countries
2. corporate income taxes	Canada generally higher than other OECD countries
3. consumption taxes (GST)	Canada generally lower than other OECD countries
4. payroll taxes (E.I. etc.)	Canada very low amongst OECD countries

Based on this data, many, including officials from the federal Department of Finance, argued that the GST should be increased and personal income taxes reduced. The logic was impeccable. The problem was, in political terms this was not a viable option for our government. We would have been lambasted by the Canadian public, NGO's and the media if we had proposed such an option. Good policy - bad politics. Interestingly, in the 2006 federal election campaign, the Conservative Party of Canada, under the leadership of Stephen Harper, promised to reduce the GST by two percentage points, from 7% to 5% if they formed

---

18   Recent trends in taxes internationally; Lin, Zhengxi, Perspectives on Labour and Income, The online edition, January 2001, Volume 2, No. 1

the government. Once elected, they delivered on this promise in two stages of one percent reductions. Good politics - bad policy.

The Harmonized sales Tax (HST) is another good example of where politics and policy do not intersect smoothly. Not being able to eliminate/ scrap the GST following the 1993 election, our government decided that the best available option was to try to harmonize the GST with the provincial sales tax in the provinces. The exception was Alberta which does not have a provincial sales tax. There are significant macroeconomic advantages associated with harmonizing the GST with provincial sales taxes, not the least of which are the administrative savings accruing to businesses and the provincial governments in reducing two taxes to one tax. Equally importantly, the PST, unlike the GST, is an imbedded tax from which business and individuals get no relief. With the GST, however, input credits are permitted so that tax is only on 'value-added'. This brings us more in line with our competitors and in the medium term-long term helps a provincial economy to generate more economic activity and jobs. The downside to harmonization is that services that were exempt from provincial sales taxes are now taxed when the taxes are harmonized. Herein lies the dilemma - the benefits accrue in the medium/long term, and the negative impacts, in the form of higher point-of-sale taxes on many services, begin in the short term. Mr. Pareto would have struggled with this one also. Try as we might, most of the provinces declined to harmonize with the exception of in New Brunswick, Newfoundland and Labrador, and Nova Scotia who harmonized in 1996/97 - at a combined level at that time of 13% which was lower, by design, than the aggregate of the two taxes. This latter step was a wise move designed to mitigate, à la Pareto, some of the initial negative reaction to the HST - for the reasons cited above. Ontario and British Columbia more recently harmonized their sales taxes - a move that has generated a very nasty campaign in B.C., led by former B.C. Premier Bill Vander Zalm, to eliminate the harmonized tax and revert back to the provincial sales tax. Good politics/ bad policy.

The responsibilities of Members of Parliament do not end here. In addition to the work described above in the House of Commons and in committee, there are commitments for various public speaking engagements, meeting with constituents and other special interest or stakeholder groups, attending community functions, participating in media interviews, and representing Canada abroad.

The volume of communications in various forms flowing through my offices was considerable. In Ottawa, when the House was in session, we received over 2,000 e—mails each week, 100 phone calls, 200 letters from various organizations, and about 10—20 letters a week from constituents. In a typical week we would receive 30 House of Commons/Senate and other external reports. Likewise, at my constituency office in Toronto there was a continuous flow of people, phone calls and correspondence.

As an MP I had a very strict policy of responding to people who communicated with my office within a reasonable period of time and we strove to meet this objective.

phone calls:	call back within 2—3 days.
letters:	write back within 3 weeks.
e—mails:	communicate electronically within one week.

One colleague of mine returned telephone calls to constituents every morning around 7:30 a.m. While risky, he told me that people were typically impressed with the fact that he was up and running so early in the morning!

Members of Parliament are also able to mail out four newsletters, or 'householders', per year to each and every address in his/her riding. This takes the form of a 4—6 page newsletter in which you have the opportunity to communicate directly with your constituents. I took full advantage of this opportunity to send information, unfiltered by the media or opposition parties, to tell people what local events I had attended and what my work priorities were on the hill, and what our party was doing with respect to legislation and policy. That these 'householders' were perhaps the most important way of communication became very clear to me when I visited constituents during election campaigns and on other occasions and I listened to their positive feedback. Not limited to substantive policy issues, I recall one constituent in the printing business who gave me some suggestions about fonts and format which were incorporated into the next issue.

MPs are also able to mail up to 2,000 Christmas cards each year at no charge to their budget. This became an annual ritual for me, especially writing personal notes on many of the cards thanking people for their support.

Another tool available to MPs is the "ten per center". Let me explain how this works. MPs can mail out a one page, two sided, message to 10% of their constituents on any non—partisan matter, as many times as they like. Typically, they will target a message to an area of the riding that would have a particular interest in the subject matter. For example, a federal immigration detention centre serving Lester B. Pearson Airport, was being relocated from Mississauga to my riding of Etobicoke North. As a result of some misinformation that was circulating about the detention centre, I sent a 'ten per center' into the area where the facility was to be located. The distribution of 'ten per centers' are based on postal codes and postal walks and, while time—consuming on my staff to draft the message and sort the packages by postal code, it was an effective way of targeting issues that were important to certain segments of the community. Another use was to communicate targeted positive messages. An example would be a bulletin on noise abatement enhancements at Pearson Airport directed to homes and apartments close to the airport or in aircraft flight paths.

I used these 'ten per centers' judiciously and perhaps during a year I might have sent out six or seven of them. By way of contrast, one of my colleagues from Northern Ontario told me he was in the habit of sending out one each day!

To this day there continues to be controversy over the practice of MPs sending 'ten per centers' into ridings other than their own–constituencies represented by members of another political party. In my view this has reached ridiculous proportions and needs to be reined in, although I am guilty of sending one or two 'ten per centers' into my twin riding of Saanich— Gulf Islands–hardly the flood of mail being experienced today.

Most Canadians, but certainly not all, understand that MPs are not overpaid. Out of curiosity, on one occasion I computed that on a per hour basis, my salary as an MP was technically below the minimum wage. I never complained about my compensation, because rewards came in many other forms and my salary was much higher than the average pay for Canadians generally. Plus, I had a job–one that generated a somewhat unique make—or— break performance review every two or three years in the form of elections – but an interesting and challenging job nonetheless.

Members of Parliament are currently paid an annual salary of $158,000. This is a respectable amount, but not sufficient to attract bank executives and professional athletes!

Unless legislated otherwise, salaries and allowances are adjusted annually in accordance with the index of the average percentage increase in base—rate wages for each calendar year, resulting from major settlements negotiated with bargaining units of five hundred or more employees in the private sector in Canada, as published by the Department of Human Resources Development. Additional remuneration is also available for performing various parliamentary roles. For example, the prime minister is paid an additional $158,000 annually for a total of $315,000; ministers an extra $76,000; and parliamentary secretaries an extra $16,000. The leader of the official opposition and the speaker both receive $75,000 in addition to their base salary of $158,000. Chairs of Standing, and Standing Joint Committees, of the House of Commons are paid $11,000 over and above their annual salary as an MP. There is also extra pay for party whips, caucus chairs and others.

Up until 2000 the House of Commons had a strange and hypocritical way of paying MPs. The basic salary at that time was $68,200 per annum. To this was added an expense allowance of $12,000, and a *non—taxable* expense allowance of $22,500. This compensation package was 'smoke and mirrors' taken to new heights! Vouchers or receipts were not required to justify the $22,500 allowance–it was simply paid out to MPs. The net effect of this was to understate the salaries of MPs by some $30,000 (when the tax free allowance and expense allowance are measured on a before—income tax basis)!

The Liberal government wanted to change this anomaly and increase the transparency of MP compensation. With the support of the House of Commons in the year 2001 the tax free allowance and the additional expense allowances were eliminated and the annual salary for MPs in that year became an all—inclusive taxable amount of $131,400. This system is still in place and is a vast improvement in pay reporting. Interestingly, in another example of politics at its worst, when the Liberal government proposed this change to the other political parties in the House, they all agreed – only to argue against it in the House of Commons Chamber and vote against it. Fortunately the majority Liberal government ruled the day and the bill passed. Opposition parties were hypocritical in the extreme in their attempt to counter their concern that average Canadians would view the change as a salary increase for MPs–which it was clearly not.

A pension is paid to a former Member who has made contributions for at least six (6) years and who has been elected to the House of Commons at least twice. The pension cannot be collected until the Member is at least fifty— five years of age. A Member's annual retirement allowance is based on the number of years the Member paid into his or her pension and is calculated based on the average annual sessional allowance over the best five consecutive years of service (five consecutive years of highest—paid pensionable service).

At age 60, a Member's Retiring Allowance is indexed annually to reflect changes in the cost of living. The following table shows that the average annual allowance (i.e. pension), including indexation, was $48,985 for former members of the House of Commons and $55,012 for former members of the Senate.

Table – Pensions for Members of Parliament Distribution of Annual Allowances in Pay (including applicable indexation) at March 31, 2008				
Amount of Allowance ($)	Former Members	Survivors	Dependant Children/Students	Total
70,000 and over	80	–	–	80
65,000–69,999	23	1	–	24
60,000–64,999	44	–	–	44
55,000–59,999	27	1	–	28
50,000–54,999	30	1	–	31
45,000–49,999	32	3	–	35
40,000–44,999	43	13	–	56
35,000–39,999	48	26	–	74
30,000–34,999	38	9	–	47
25,000–29,999	21	24	–	45
20,000–24,999	31	22	–	53
15,000–19,999	21	18	–	39
10,000–14,999	17	23	–	40
5,000–9,999	16	13	4	33
Up to 4,999	–	–	1	1
Totals	**471**	**154**	**5**	**630**

Notes:

Included in the above allowances, two former members were in receipt of an indexed annual allowance for service as prime minister.

The average annual allowance, including indexation, was $55,012 for former members of the Senate and $48,985 for former members of the House of Commons.

There were 14 former members of the Senate and 66 former members of the House of Commons who received an annual pension, including indexing and MPRCA, exceeding $70,000

Source: Treasury Board of Canada Secretariat : Report on the Administration of the Members of Parliament Retiring Allowances Act for the Fiscal Year Ended March 31, 2008

I served as parliamentary secretary to two different ministers, and as chair of the standing committee on finance, and as vice—chair of both the standing committee on public safety and national security and the standing committee on transportation, and my pension, after twelve and one half years of service in the House of Commons is respectable and higher than the 2008 average for all retired MPs, but not even close to the amounts bandied about by the press. Fortunately I have other assets that I can draw down to augment my pension income. The 'gold plated' description attributed to MPs pensions invariably refers to MPs who have served for twenty years or more and who have been in Cabinet for perhaps half of that time. But I am not complaining. Some Canadians have no pension other that the Old Age Security and the Canada Pension Plan, and a number of underfunded private sector pension plans are currently threatened by companies who have gone into bankruptcy protection or been declared bankrupt.

The 'perks' that go hand—in—hand with the life of an MP go beyond compensation and living allowances. Canadians, individuals and corporations alike, are known to shower MPs with small gifts and complimentary invitations to a multitude of functions. While most of these are magnanimous gestures of thanks or respect, one has to ensure that all such acts of generosity comply with rules established by Canada's Parliamentary *Conflict of Interest and Ethics Commissioner*. Over my years as MP I have been on the receiving end of the following types of ethically compliant 'freebies' –

- baseball, hockey and basketball tickets;
- meals at restaurants and banquets;
- concerts;
- bottles of wine, scotch and cognac at Christmastime; and,
- golf tournaments.

Traveling as an MP can often result in special treatment–such as being whisked to the airport V.I.P. lounge prior to departure, being checked in by lounge staff and then driven to the aircraft where you climb a set of stairs to the aircraft cabin entrance and directly to your seat. On arrival you are met at the bottom of the aircraft ramp, driven to the V.I.P. lounge where you sip a tea or coffee while someone processes you through Customs & Immigration and collects your baggage. Ah, the good life!

When I worked in the private sector with the Noranda Forest Group (Norbord) my benefits included a company car, annual bonus, membership in a private club, and other 'perks' which were different, and not truly comparable to my House of Commons experience. For corporate work I often traveled with the company president (first class) and stayed in luxurious hotels - like the Goring Hotel in London, England which the Middleton family took over for the wedding of Catherine and William in April 2011 so they could be close to Buckingham Palace.

I recall one 'perk' as an MP that was particularly enjoyable. A company in my riding that had four season tickets to the Toronto Raptor NBA basketball team, called one day and told me the four tickets were mine if I could use them. I contacted a local organization—the **Albion Neighborhood Services Boys and Girls Club** whose mission is "to provide a safe, supportive place where children and youth can experience new opportunities, overcome barriers, build positive relationships and develop confidence and skills for life"[19]. I invited two young people, together with a Boys & Girls Club counselor, to join me for the basketball game between the Toronto Raptors and the Boston Celtics. A counselor chose two boys and the four of us were off to the game. The tickets were in the platinum section and I noted that the value of each ticket was $350! Our seats were almost at court level and very close to the Celtics bench. The two boys were ecstatic, and they were very well behaved and extremely appreciative. I think it was a memory that they will never forget (nor will I!). My faith in today's youth was restored after that evening–and I felt that the gift of tickets had been used well.

When Labatt's closed its brewery in Etobicoke North in 2005 to consolidate its Ontario production in London, Ontario, the beer company set up a scholarship in my name at Humber Institute of Technology and Advanced Learning. Their $100,000 donation was matched by the Ontario Government for a total permanent endowment of $200,000 which funds tuition scholarships (one or two scholarships depending on the endowment income) to deserving students who –

- are graduating from a high school in Etobicoke;
- achieving superior academic results;
- are in need of financial assistance; and
- have a record of community service.

---

19   Boys and Girls Clubs of Canada web site

Every year, in perpetuity, I will be invited to Humber College to personally make the award presentation. In my absence, someone from the College performs this honour in my place.

I am very proud of this community 'legacy' and grateful to Labatt's for making this happen. Many students in Etobicoke have, and will, benefit from this generous gesture by Labatt's and the Ontario Provincial Government.

Another modest legacy of mine that I am very happy about is a tree that I planted, together with an engraved plaque at the base of the tree, in 1998 at St. Philip's Anglican Church in Etobicoke North on the occasion of their 170th anniversary. In 1828, St. Philip's Church and Churchyard were established on the west side of the Humber River, making the church the second oldest church in Toronto. The 170th anniversary was celebrated in the church yard on a beautifully sunny day. I read a congratulatory message from Prime Minister Jean Chrétien and left the letter with the congregation. Later on, I planted the tree, which grows taller each year. It was no coincidence that St. Philip's Church was the church in Toronto that my wife Ethne and I attended. All future trips to Etobicoke will include a visit to St. Philips to see Reverend Allan Budzin, his wife Julie, members of the congregation—and the tree of course!

On the opposition bench

A number of my Liberal colleagues in the House of Commons were elected in 1988 and served on the opposition benches until the 1993 general election at which time our Party formed the government. Many of them, like Stan Keyes and Joe Fontana, told me they had really enjoyed being in opposition during those years because there was less stress and fewer responsibilities. It also provided them with the opportunity to get acquainted with how parliament works, and with what tools opposition members have at their disposal. They believe that this experience prepared them well for the government benches and was a great way to phase into life in Ottawa.

When I was elected in the 1996 by—election I went directly to the government side of the House as part of a majority government. For ten years I was able to participate in government decision—making and to interact directly with ministers and the prime minister who were my caucus colleagues. I was in for a shock in 2006 when we lost the election and were relegated to the opposition benches. My role was no longer one of assisting with the development of government policy, but rather to pick holes and weaknesses in the policies of the Conservative government. I found this to be less interesting and not as challenging – especially since my experience had been up until then as part of the government. Ideally a stint in opposition before moving to the government side is a good way to sequence things, but we usually can't control this and having any seat in the House of Commons is a privilege and honour at any time.

Three of my former colleagues, Sheila Copps, Don Boudria, and John Nunziata became affectionately to be known as the 'rat pack' in opposition, where they were highly effective in attacking the Conservative Government of Brian Mulroney and in keeping it off balance and 'off message'. I never found such a niche.

There are various tools available to MPs when in opposition. Some of these are the following –

- oral questions during Question Period;
- Adjournment Proceedings ('late show');
- Questions on the Order Paper;
- Access to Information requests; and,
- engaging the media.

Making it onto the list for an oral question for Question Period can be a daunting task, even for an opposition critic. There are only so many questions and supplementary questions per party. The Leader of the Official Opposition most often presents the first three questions. The questions typically concern some hot topic of the day and are designed to have the biggest political impact. The Government Opposition Leader in the House of Commons, which during my time was Hon. Ralph Goodale, P.C., M.P., orchestrates the Official Opposition Party priorities and sequencing of questions for the daily Question Period, which starts every sitting day at 2:15 p.m., except for Fridays when it begins at 11:15 a.m. It lasts for forty—five minutes. Once the questions are chosen, we had a practice session before QP each day at which time adherence to the thirty five second limit was reinforced and content and delivery fine—tuned.

Another useful tool is the Adjournment proceedings, also referred to as the "late show". During QP, if you are not satisfied with the answer you had from the Minister, you can , within a stipulated time period, complete a form and hand it to a Page in the House Chamber requesting an adjournment proceeding. The Minister or his/her Parliamentary Secretary must work with you and establish a mutually agreeable date and time for a "late show". These are held from 6:30 p.m. to 7:00 p.m. Monday through Thursday, after which the House adjourns. This debate, which runs for a maximum of 30 minutes, allows for brief exchanges between Members and Ministers or Parliamentary Secretaries as a follow—up to QP.

An example of a question posed during Question Period, and the follow—up during a Late Show is provided in Appendix 1.

If one cannot make it to the roster for Question Period in a timely manner, or if the question involves a lengthy, detailed or technical response, a written question can always be placed on the *Order Paper* after giving forty—eight hours written notice to the clerk. There are certain requirements covering the form and content of such questions and an MP may have a maximum of four questions on the *Order Paper* at any one time. If requested, the government is required to respond to the question within forty—five sitting days. Should the government fail to respond within the forty—five day time limit, the matter is automatically referred to the relevant Standing Committee where the Chair of the Committee is obliged to call a meeting of the committee, or place this item on the committee agenda, to deal with this failure to comply with the House rules.

In opposition, I used this technique on a number of occasions. Often the answers, not confined to a thirty—five second answer as they would be during Oral Question Period, were more fulsome and complete. I would also make a simultaneous *Access to Information* request on the same topic to provide myself with greater assurance that the Government was not attempting to hide anything. Canada's *Access to Information Act* requires the Government or agency to respond within thirty days after paying a fee of five dollars.

When we became Her Majesty's Loyal Opposition, commonly known as the Official Opposition, in 2006, Hon. Bill Graham, P.C., was our interim leader. I was flattered and thrilled when Bill asked me to serve in his shadow cabinet as Critic for Natural Resources. I have always admired and respected Bill and therefore I accepted the role without hesitation. I felt also that it was a good fit for me, having worked before I was elected in the forest sector and in the Noranda Group.

My first task as critic was to meet with all the major stakeholder groups – organizations like the Forest Products Association of Canada, The National Roundtable on the Environment & the Economy, The Canadian Wind Energy Association, the Mining Association of Canada, Pollution Probe, the Canadian Association of Petroleum Producers, the Canadian Electricity Association, to name a few. In our one—on—one discussions, I indicated I was interested in understanding some of the challenges and opportunities within the natural resource sector. As a result of these meetings, and after consulting with caucus colleagues, I decided to focus on the following issues–

- the need for a national energy strategy which emphasized renewable energy within the overall mix of energy choices;
- structural problems in the mining and forestry sectors; and,
- sustainable oil sands development.

The Conservative Minister of Natural Resources at the time was Hon. Gary Lunn, P.C., the MP representing Saanich—Gulf Islands in British Columbia. I was very familiar with this riding, having lived there in the late 1980's and, as the MP for Etobicoke North, I was 'twinned' with this riding. My responsibilities with the twin riding were to provide a channel of communication for the federal Liberal riding Association in that area; to listen to their views on government directions and priorities; to brief them on the government legislative strategy and political strategies; and, finally, to help them in their mission to elect a Liberal MP in Saanich—Gulf Islands.

On numerous occasions, during Question Period I asked the Minister if there was a national energy strategy, and if not there should be. I was told many times that such a strategy was under development but I, for one, am still waiting. I believe the Conservative government is very nervous about enunciating a strategy that might be associated with the very politically divisive national energy program that the Liberal government announced in1980. A strategy is needed, I believe, to address such key issues as energy security and responsible resource development that is environmentally sustainable. I find it curious, and frankly hypocritical, that our American friends and neighbours speak of the need for a continental approach to energy, because it is in their interest to do so, whereas with softwood lumber, which is bought and sold within a very integrated North American market, the US Congress takes a different approach. While I understand why our American allies wish to reduce their dependency on middle eastern oil, and why it is very natural for them to look north for an alternative supply, I have argued with them directly that if the development of, and production from, the Alberta oil sands is part of this solution, the US needs to partner with Canada in finding the ways to address the significant environmental challenges associated with this strategy.

The environmental challenges, in my view, are threefold –

1. soaring production of CO_2 at a time when climate change is dictating that there should be significant reductions of same;
2. overuse of water resources in the Athabasca River Basin; and,
3. lowest and worst use of scarce natural gas energy to extract, upgrade and refine the bitumen found in the oil sands.

We should be reducing our dependency on fossil fuels and moving towards renewable energy sources. I accept the reality, however, that in the short—medium term there will still be a large demand for oil and gas that will need to be met. Carbon capture and sequestration is a technology that, if technically and economically feasible, could go a long way to reducing or eliminating CO_2 emissions from the oil sands. Governments and industry, on both sides of the border, need to partner to do the research needed to accelerate the development and deployment of carbon capture technologies. We aren't there yet.

While the proponents of the oil sands argue that the huge amounts of water used to extract the bitumen are recycled back into the Athabasca River, this is only partly true. We need to speed up the development and deployment of these water recycling technologies here too so that all users of this water resource – farmers, aboriginal Canadians, fishers – are protected.

Finally, why we are using cleaner and much sought out natural gas in the oil sands extraction and production processes is a mystery to me. We need to look at alternatives, including nuclear power, and direct our precious natural gas to better uses – such as home heating, manufacturing plants, and feedstock for Canada's petrochemical industry.

All of these issues are within the context of a physical and social infrastructure in the Fort McMurray area that are stretched to the limits, and in some cases beyond.

Why not slow down the development of the oil sands until such time as we can proceed in a sustainable manner? The bitumen will always be there. With development costs soaring as a result of excess demand, the economic argument becomes as powerful as the environmental one.

Former Alberta Premier, Peter Lougheed, was more aligned with the people of Alberta than the federal Conservatives when he argued for a slowdown in the development of the oil sands.

I questioned the Conservative government's position on the oil sands on a number of occasions – including questions in Question Period – to no avail. Sanctimonious and superficial answers were the order of the day on this topic and this continues.

I pushed for a review of oil sands development by the House of Commons Standing Committee on Natural Resources. This we did and we issued a report entitled *OIL SANDS: TOWARD SUSTAINABLE DEVELOPMENT* following a visit to Fort McMurray and a tour of the oil sands and meetings with oil sands executives and other stakeholders.

The oil sands issue generated some challenges within the Liberal caucus and had to be treated very carefully so as not to generate any 'western alienation'. Although we had no MPs from Alberta at that time, the Alberta Senators kept me on my toes!

As the Opposition Critic for Natural Resources, I also argued for a continuation of the Energuide for Houses program and the wind power turbine construction incentive program—programs that our government had introduced and the Conservative government had put on hold when they came to power. There is some dialogue on this in Appendix 1.

Serving in opposition certainly was frustrating and not as rewarding and satisfying as working on the government side. With the levers of power in other hands, we had to content ourselves to speaking out as loudly and clearly as possible.

There was one particular incident that underscored for me the frustration and futility of serving on the opposition side of the House of Commons. While serving as Opposition Critic for Natural Resources, Gary Lunn, the Minister of Natural Resources, invited me to join him for meetings in Washington, D.C. Ministers often did this for two reasons – firstly to build a positive relationship between the Minister and the critic; and, secondly, and perhaps more importantly, to pair departures from the House of Commons to cancel any upcoming votes in the Chamber. The main purpose of the Minister's visit to the USA was to participate in tri—lateral discussions with his Mexican and US counterparts on a range of issues, in particular continental energy policy. My Ottawa staff was able to ascertain that I would not be able to participate in the tri—lateral meetings, but I was invited to a dinner of the Canadian American Business Council (CABC). Given these limitations, I came close to declining the invitation, but on reflection decided to put together my own program while the trilateral meetings were in progress. As a result, I was able to conduct some very successful meetings with Members of the US House of Representatives, US Senators, and US think tanks and learn much about energy policy and programs.

When the time for the dinner arrived, we assembled at a very posh private club in central Washington DC and after a short reception with cocktails, we took our places at the dinner table. There were about fifteen business leaders in attendance, and individuals like Gordon Giffin, former Ambassador of the United States to Canada. A short welcome from the executive director of the CABC followed, and then those seated at the dinner table were asked to say a few words by way of introduction. This is when I started to feel sick. Almost all of those present made very flattering statements directed to Minister Lunn about the early performance of his government. Some of the positive comments were accompanied by subtle digs at the Government of Paul Martin, of which I was part. Fortunately, former Ambassador Giffin, perhaps gauging my body language and understanding diplomacy, came to the rescue and altered the direction of the conversation somewhat.

While this change was welcomed by me, we quickly moved into another contentious area – energy policy. All of those assembled spoke to the need for the US to reduce its dependency on middle eastern oil, for obvious reasons centered around national security, and why Canada was such an obvious choice as an alternative supplier of oil and gas – in particular from the oil sands in Alberta. This train of thought continued for some time and although I agreed with the thrust of the argument I believed that one piece of the puzzle had been ignored. As an invited guest of Minister Lunn and the CABC, it was not my intent to insert any negativity to the discussion or rain on the parade of the Minister. At what I felt was the appropriate time, however, I entered the fray and agreed with the notion that Canada, as a neighbor, ally, and friend to the United States, was a logical supply source for oil and gas—with one caveat. Canada and the United States, if we were to be partners in energy development and Middle East supply displacement, needed to work together to address the many environmental issues associated with the oil sands. I outlined these issues briefly—reducing CO^2 emissions, recycling the water, and finding a source other than natural gas to extract the bitumen.

Minister Lunn was the first to respond to my comments by agreeing with my concerns, and then by pointing out, in what seemed to me to be a very superficial and cavalier way, that all the CO^2 would be captured and sequestered, and all of the water would be recycled. He would make sure of that. I replied, being careful not to dominate the discussion, that if that was the direction he was headed in I, together with my Liberal Party colleagues, would be behind him one hundred per cent. However, I pointed out, it was one thing to have an idea and goal – and often quite another matter to actually implement something that was technically and economically feasible. His government is still struggling with these challenges and progress remains slow. This dinner meeting proved one thing to me. Our Party had to get back into power. Being in opposition was really horrible!

Home is Ottawa

The House of Commons typically sits from mid—September until mid—December and then from the end of January until mid June. Weeks in Ottawa are scheduled for 2—3 weeks in a row followed by one week for MP's to stay in their ridings and deal with constituency matters. These weeks in the riding usually are centered around important national holidays like Canada Day at which time MP's have a variety of events to attend.

In twelve years as a federal MP, I tried different types of accommodation – my last abode being the bottom floor of a duplex which I rented about fifteen minutes away from the Hill. I walked to and from my office every day in Ottawa. I enjoyed having my own entrance and the ability to leave my possessions in Ottawa year round. When first elected in 1996, I stayed in a hotel that catered to MPs and Senators and was close to the Hill. The problem with that was the need to check out on Fridays and check in again on Monday the following week. After 3—4 years of hotel living I shared a condo with another Liberal MP, but this turned out to be more like college dorm living so I finally zeroed in on a duplex. The only challenge with the duplex was that I was responsible for keeping it cleaned, so with the hours I kept in Ottawa, Molly Maids come to the rescue.

MPs approach the challenge of accommodation in Ottawa in very different ways, depending on the location of their riding, their family situation, and other factors. Some MPs with a spouse and young children and a riding some distance from Ottawa may decide to purchase a home in Ottawa and this is where the whole family settles. Children are enrolled in Ottawa schools and the family establishes itself in the Ottawa area. The advantage of this arrangement is that the MP is able to have more time with his/her spouse and children. The challenge with this option is making sure that enough evenings and weekends are spent in the riding meeting with constituents and attending events and functions. The visibility of the MP in the riding must be maintained at acceptable levels, otherwise voters will quickly turn to another candidate who is willing to make this commitment and deliver on it. I have always been of the view that the most difficult situation is an MP whose riding is distant from Ottawa and who has a young family.

Can you imagine, for example, the challenges facing an MP with a young family representing a riding in Prince George, British Columbia. To travel home Friday afternoon after the House of Commons recesses for the weekend would require a flight from Ottawa to Toronto, Toronto to Vancouver and then Vancouver to Prince George. There are only a very few direct flights from Ottawa to Vancouver. The total flying time would be about six hours, and together with airport connection time, an arrival in Prince George at about midnight Friday night would be about the best one could do. If the MP had business in the House on Monday, this would call for traveling on flights virtually all day Sunday to return to Ottawa because of the added problem of the loss of three hours due to the movement through time zones. Alternatively, the 'red eye' leaving Vancouver around midnight Sunday would place you in Ottawa reasonably early Monday morning. These scenarios assume no travel delays and with our Canadian winters this is not always possible. Fortunately, it is sometimes possible to skip Monday in Ottawa and return for Tuesday morning, but this very much depends on what is happening in the House, in caucus, and one's unique responsibilities and interests.

Given the punishing travel demands, it is not difficult to understand why the families of some MPs move to Ottawa. Invariably, however, this step must be accompanied by available accommodation in the riding— either keeping one's own residence, or staying with friends/relatives, or booking into an hotel – for those frequent occasions when one's presence in the riding to attend meetings or functions is required.

It is an interesting phenomenon that has developed on the Hill over time and that is the trading of days in Ottawa with other caucus colleagues. So, for example, if I am able to stay in Ottawa on a Friday, but I would like to be in my riding on Monday, but I am required to be in Ottawa on Monday to be on house duty, I may trade with a colleague who is needed in Ottawa for house duty on Friday with commitments in his/her riding on that day, but available to be in Ottawa on Monday. In this way one colleague covers for the other and vice versa. These 'swaps' are recorded in the Whip's office so that there is no confusion around who will be present for house duty.

Other types of 'swaps' are common, for example covering for a colleague who has a clash with an important meeting of a Standing Committee and other responsibilities in the riding or in Ottawa. Again, the whip's office would be notified who is attending the committee meeting in lieu of the permanent member. There are some risks associated with committee meeting trades that need to be managed to ensure that the person who is substituting for you will not 'break rank' with your position at the Committee meeting and cause a loss of cohesion in your and/ or your caucus' view of relevant bills or studies. This usually calls for a review of the committee meeting agenda in advance, and a discussion with one's replacement prior to the swap if any contentious matters are in the offing.

According to House of Commons rules, in any budget year I could travel anywhere in Canada, and four times to Washington, DC, up to a maximum of 64 total round trips per year. I was provided with a telephone card which allowed me to use a House of Commons trunk line and unlimited phone calls anywhere in the world at any time. A $30,000 annual allowance for my living expenses when I was in Ottawa covered my rental accommodation and a small per diem allowance for meals and incidentals.

The conventional wisdom is that being an MP can be tough on family life – and it can be, especially those living far away from Ottawa and those with young families. Fortunately for me, my loving and supporting wife Ethne had a career of her own in Toronto, and when I first ran for elected office our son was twenty years old. Nonetheless, we all took great pains to stay in touch with each other and I would call my wife from Ottawa every evening from my office or once I had returned to my abode in Ottawa. Speaking on the telephone, however, is a far cry from being together. Comparing my situation to other MPs who lived far away from Ottawa made me realize that their challenges were more severe than mine. I recall a colleague who represented a riding in Saskatchewan who had to fly to Regina, via Toronto, and then travel by car from Regina for two hours, often in bitter winter weather, to his home, arriving typically in the wee hours of the morning after leaving Ottawa in the late afternoon.

This is why some MPs located at great distance from Ottawa move their families to Ottawa to minimize the travel time back and forth to their ridings. Not being as visible in the riding, however, introduces some political risk, recognizing that voters like to have easy access to their elected officials. In my riding of Etobicoke North, weekend political events in the riding typically required my attendance at 3—4 different functions. Missing these events, over time, would have been at some political cost – and this is the dilemma facing MPs who take up residence in Ottawa. Having one's family together is a strong motivator and often rightly overrides the political downsides.

Edward Bates, the United States Attorney General under Abraham Lincoln from 1861 to 1864, had this to say about being separated from his wife when he first won a seat in the U.S. House of Representatives many years earlier in 1827 –

".......''a plague upon the vanity of petty ambition! Were I great enough to sway the destinies of the nation, the mead of ambition might be worth the sacrifice which it requires; but a mere seat in Congress as a subaltern member, is a contemptible price for the happiness which we enjoy with each other..."[20]

Evenings in Ottawa would often find me in the Chamber of the House of Commons until 6:30p.m. or later. Reaching my home in Ottawa before 9 p.m. was a rare occurrence. After leaving the chamber I would attend a caucus meeting and/or briefing; or catch up with work in my office after a day of running around attending meetings; or meet over dinner with constituents who were visiting Ottawa; or with national business leaders to discuss topical public policy issues.

Recess periods away from Parliament are always less demanding, and, as a result, they provide MPs the opportunity to re-charge their batteries and prepare for the next session. From mid-December until the end of January each year, time is spent on holiday political functions and for family holiday time. Of course, catching up with constituents who have been in the queue waiting for you to return from Ottawa is a key priority during these six weeks. Our Liberal caucus, and other party caucuses, typically meet for a couple of days, in rotating cities, prior to returning to Ottawa at the end of January. These sessions are used to assess the state of the political landscape and to solidify tactics for the upcoming session. Likewise, the summer recess, from mid June until mid September, is used by most MPs to take some down time, mixed in with political meetings, events and functions, and in my case – golf! There is always a summer

---

20   Goodwin, Doris Kearns, Team of Rivals, Simon & Shuster, New York, NY, 2005, page 64

caucus meeting in a different location in Canada that runs for two-three days at which time polling data is reviewed, new initiatives are discussed, and political strategies are hatched.

Often during the summer recess I would select a few areas of my riding at random and I would canvass the area. This often surprised people, sometimes sitting out on their lawns or working their gardens, and frequently caused them to ask if there was an election in progress. Answering no, I would then ask them if there were any issues that they would like to discuss with me, or information they would like me to know about. Another advantage of doing this work - I could always reply with honesty at election time that I had been out and about knocking on doors in the riding throughout my mandate when accused sometimes of only showing up at people's doors during election campaigns to ask for their vote.

In the summer of 1998, as Chair of the Ontario Caucus, with the very capable support of Nikki Macdonald from the Liberal Research Bureau, I organized a two day retreat in the Muskokas north of Toronto where we developed a document which spelled out what the policy and program priorities were for the members of the largest Liberal caucus, by far, at the time - the Ontario Caucus. I presented this report to the full national caucus later that summer and also met one-on-one with Prime Minister Chrétien to take him through our report. We were motivated to prepare this report to ensure that there were no ambiguities surrounding what course the Ontario Liberal MPs and Senators thought the federal government should chart. I believe it had an impact and resulted in a number of our priorities addressed in the next Speech from the Throne.

Members of Parliament are drawn from all walks of life. There are former teachers, lawyers, doctors, media professionals, small business operators, and even some accountants like me. Getting used to how Ottawa works and how big and cumbersome the bureaucracy is does not come easily to everyone. My seven year stint as an Assistant Deputy Minister in the British Columbia government prepared me to some extent for what was to follow after my first election to the House of Commons in 1996, but for some colleagues government is a whole new experience. Witness the recent batch of NDP Members of Parliament - some of whom who were totally surprised that they were elected on May 2, 2011. Their learning curve will be a steep one.

A recent study by Samara, a charitable organization that studies citizen engagement with Canadian democracy, discovered that many of us had landed in Ottawa somewhat by accident - based on their exit interviews of former MPs -

"...Few said they set out intending on a career in public life, and even many who served in local or provincial office indicated that politics was something they fell into unexpectedly. Furthermore, the road to politics is subject to chance. There was no obvious "farm team" in Canadian politics: the MPs we interviewed came to Ottawa with a wide variety of backgrounds and motivations. The ways people were approached to run, and accepted, were equally varied. The nomination process was also described as inconsistent and often confusing. This report contains many examples of how such experiences turned these MPs into "accidental" citizens..."[21]

In 2000, Wajid Khan, a Pakistani-Canadian, owned and operated a successful car dealership in Toronto. I kept bumping into Wajid at functions at the International Muslim Organization (IMO). He was a big supporter of this Mosque in my riding and was very often asked to speak at events there. As I got to know him better, we began to discuss politics and he told me that he was very impressed with Paul Martin as Finance Minister. When Paul Martin ran for the leadership of the Liberal Party I encouraged Wajid to join the Martin campaign, and an introductory meeting with Paul Martin was arranged. Wajid was a great help to Paul with financial contributions and also by virtue of Wajid's high profile within the Pakistani-Canadian community - especially in the Toronto area where he had a large following for his radio program. With an election looming in 2004, there was an opening for a Liberal candidate in Mississauga-Streetsville. I encouraged him to run. He was elected with over 50% support in that election. Along with Yasmin Ratansi, Wajid was the first Muslim Member of Parliament (MP) to be elected for the Liberal Party.

Shortly after Wajid arrived in Ottawa, he became aware of an issue that I had been working on for some time. A Canadian aerospace company who had sold close-in-weapon-systems to the Pakistani Navy was trying to return these weapons to Pakistan following their repair and refurbishment in Canada. Between the time that the weapons had been sold to Pakistan and the time they were about to be returned, Canada had imposed, along with many other countries, a ban on the export of offensive weapons to Pakistan. A close-in weapon system (CIWS), often pronounced *sea-whiz*, is a naval shipboard point-defense weapon for detecting and destroying

---

21   Samara, The Accidental Citizen, June 2010

at short range incoming anti-ship missiles and enemy aircraft which have penetrated the outer defenses. Nearly all classes of modern warship are equipped with some kind of CIWS device[22]. While CIWS are clearly defensive weapons, they were nevertheless defined and banned for export to Pakistan to Canada.

Wajid approached me one day with the news that he had become aware of this matter and believed that this was a 'no-brainer' to fix. Given Wajid's military experience in Pakistan, and his new role as Canadian MP, this problem was a natural fit for him. The weapons had been repaired and were ready to be shipped. An export permit was needed by the Canadian aerospace company so that they could deliver the goods, and an invoice for about $6 million, to the Pakistan Navy. Without the export permit, nothing would happen. I indicated my agreement with Wajid and his frustration that this should have been resolved relatively easily, but that I had been working on this, by virtue of my personal friendship with the president of the Canadian company and the merits of the case, for about one year off and on, and it was mired in interdepartmental politics. The three federal departments of National Defense, Foreign Affairs, and International Trade were bouncing this around like a political football. No one wanted to touch it. I wished Wajid God-speed (Allah in his case!) and offered my continuing support as and when needed. He told me he would have this one wrestled to the floor in a few weeks. Given his experience running a medium-sized business, where he was the boss, he was used to a 'command and control' management style - an approach out of reach for a newly minted backbencher. Some months later I checked in with Wajid and enquired about the status of the CIWS. He was angry and frustrated with the lack of progress. Welcome to Ottawa, I thought. The matter was finally resolved, but not until 2006, thanks to the perseverance of the then Minister of International Trade, Jim Peterson. The repaired weapons were finally shipped back to the Pakistan Navy much to the relief of the Canadian company, and to Wajid and me.

One experiences many memorable events as an MP in Ottawa. In 2000, when Mr. Chrétien was Prime Minister, the Speaker of the House of Commons invited the remaining World War I veterans to Ottawa for a reception in the Speaker's Salon. This happened during the period when Joe Clark had been elected leader of the Progressive Party of Canada but had yet to secure a seat in the House of Commons. The veterans, who were

---

22   Wikipedia

few in number and all around one hundred years of age, sat in the Speaker's gallery for Question Period and then proceeded to the Salon. Many stairs were involved to reach the Salon, and none of the vets were moving too quickly. I wandered over to the Speaker's salon following Question Period to pay my respects to those remaining men and women who had fought for Canada in the great war. One veteran had made it to the salon by the time I arrived. Mr. Chrétien walked in and went over to the elderly gentleman and extended his arm for a hand shake. The old veteran remained still and did not respond to the Prime Minister's gesture.

"I'm waiting for Joe Clark", he asserted giving away his obvious Progressive Conservative leanings.

Always quick on his feet Mr. Chrétien replied, "I am waiting for Joe Clark too!" By this of course the PM meant that he was waiting for Joe Clark to take a seat in the House of Commons. I almost cracked up but pulled myself away so as not to show any disrespect for the fine, but perhaps somewhat rude, veteran. Interestingly, the last Canadian WWI veteran John Babcock died in 2010, at 109 years of age.

Rules governing hospitality expenses are clearly, or should I say somewhat clearly, spelled out in the *Conflict of Interest Code for Members of the House of Commons*. A gift may be accepted "if received as a normal expression of courtesy or protocol, or within the customary standards of hospitality that normally accompany the Member's position".[23] In addition, gifts accepted exceeding $500 in value must be disclosed to the Conflict of Interest and Ethics Commissioner in a statement "disclosing the nature of the gifts or other benefits, their source and the circumstances under which they were given."[24]

I complied with all of the provisions of the Conflict of Interest Code but from time—to—time the interpretations provided by the Office of the Conflict of Interest and Ethics Commissioner's office were confusing to me. Two examples come to mind. On one occasion a large Canadian telecommunications firm, with whom I had had no dealings heretofore, offered me 2 tickets to the Grey Cup Championship football game, which was being held in Ottawa that year. Guestimating that the value of these tickets would exceed $500, I asked my staff to seek the advice of the staff at the Ethics Commissioner's office. They advised against my attendance on the basis that at such an auspicious event there would be precious little time

---

23   Conflict of Interest Code for Members of the House of Commons (Canada), Section 14.2

24   Ibid Section 14.3

to discuss any business! I reluctantly heeded this advice but my thinking was that not discussing any business would have been seen as an argument in favour of my participation.

On another occasion, a company invited my wife and me to the National Arts Centre and Opera Lyra's annual Black and White Ball fundraiser which raises over $400,000 each year for local cultural and musical events in Ottawa. I had attended this event for a number of years, but with changes in the Conflict of Interest Code, I decided to seek the opinion of the Ethics Commissioner. They initially advised against my attendance but I told my staff not to immediately decline the invitation, but to wait until the Ethics Commissioner's Office was inundated with similar requests—some from Ministers—which I was sure would follow. Sure enough, a week later, the call came from the Office of the Ethics Commissioner reversing their earlier advice, as I had anticipated. A good time, for a good cause, was had by all!

The Conflict of Interest and Ethics Commissioner requires all MPs to file an annual disclosure or Profile outlining assets, liabilities and sources of income other than from the House of Commons. My wife, much to her chagrin, also had to comply with this as well. During my two terms as parliamentary secretary, I was required to place my investment portfolio assets into a blind trust administered by an arm's length lawyer of my choice. As parliamentary secretary to Finance Minister Paul Martin, I was required to divest of my shares in Canadian financial institutions and pressure was applied, without success, for my wife to establish a blind trust for her investments as well. In the end my wife and I agreed not to discuss the markets, interest rates, etc., given the volume of sensitive and confidential information that was available to me.

Complying with the rules of the House, and using good political judgement, may not be one and the same. Although my conscience is clear, I suffered an error of judgement when I accepted an invitation by Labatt's to Super Bowl XXXVII in January 2003 in San Diego California. It was an amazing experience and a way for Labatt's to thank me for my work as Chair of the Brewing Industry Caucus. With both Molson's and Labatt's having large breweries in my riding, employing a large number of my constituents, to me it was a 'no—brainer' to be very interested in reasonable federal issues affecting the beer industry. Following the trip to San Diego, I complied with the requirement to report my sponsored travel to the Clerk of the House of Commons. The National Post, following their usual scan of such trips looking for 'muck' ran a 'one day wonder' article about the trip and that was the end of the matter.

Interestingly, two years previously, in 2001, when I was serving as parliamentary secretary to Finance Minister Paul Martin, I had been asked by Labatt's if I would accompany them to New Orleans for Super Bowl XXXVI which was to be played in New Orleans in February 2002. While tempting I indicated that as parliamentary secretary to the Minister of Finance I would have to decline the invitation on the basis of conflict—of—interest knowing that from time—to—time excise taxes on beer came under review by the Department of Finance and the Minister and me.

"Don't worry", I was told, "We are inviting the Finance Minister as well."

"Very well", I said, "If he accepts, I will join you."

I said this knowing full well that the Finance Minister would never accept – and he didn't. Another opportunity lost – until 2003.

In 2009, the House of Commons in Great Britain came under siege as a result of an MP expense scandal characterized by the flagrant and sometimes gross misuse of the expenses system for personal gain by many MPs, including Government ministers, and across all parties. These expenditures included such items as building a moat, gardening, piano—tuning, bedding and upholstery, a subscription to the Playboy Channel, and a small floating house for ducks.

It was astounding to me that the United Kingdom, which is the original Westminster democratic parliamentary system of government adopted later by many countries, including Canada, would tolerate abuses that are not allowed in Canada's House of Commons. The following quotation from a newspaper in England, illustrates the point—

...."veteran civil servant Sir Christopher Kelly provoked a Commons backlash after calling for a ban on MPs employing spouses and relatives. He recommended that MPs should in future be required to rent, rather than buy, their second homes and that should they not be allowed to claim for properties in London if they lived within commuting distance of Westminster"[25].

In the House of Commons in Canada there are rules governing the employment of family members by MPs. In the *Conflict of Interest Act* which applies to public office holders including Ministers, Secretaries of State and Parliamentary Secretaries and specified Ministerial staff in Part 1,

---

25   Nigel Morris, Speaker Warns MPs: Don't try to water down tough reform of expenses, The Independent, November 16, 2009, page 2

(Prohibited activities while holding office) section 14 specifies that "entering into a contract or employment relationship, in the exercise of one's official duties, with a spouse, common—law partner, child, sibling or parent or permitting the entity for which one works to do so"[26], is not permitted.

Under House of Commons rules, MPs are not allowed to employ their spouses or children —

".....Members may enter into contracts for services with individuals, agencies or organizations and use a portion of the Member's Office Budget for the payment of these contractors. Members may not hire or enter into a contract for consulting and professional services with members of their immediate family (spouses and children and their spouses and children)"[27].

While there is nothing to stop MPs from hiring family members of their caucus colleagues and paying them from their parliamentary budgets, In the Conflict of Interest Code for Members of the House of Commons, the following section (8) under Rules of Conduct (Furthering private interests) provides general guidance and as a result only a handful of MPs have family members of caucus colleagues on staff —

> **8.** When performing parliamentary duties and functions, a Member shall not act in any way to further his or her private interests or those of a member of the Member's family, or to improperly further another person's or entity's private interests"[28].

With respect to housing allowances, Doug Ward of the Vancouver Sun summarizes the key differences very succinctly –

"A key difference between the Canadian and British systems involves housing costs incurred by MPs while living away from their homes in the country's capital —— an expense that is at the heart of the British scandal. In Britain, MPs are allowed to claim expenses on second homes on the grounds that the politicians need a home in London near Parliament as well as in their home constituency.

26   *Conflict of Interest Act* (Canada)

27   House of Commons Procedure and Practice, Edited by Robert Marleau and Camille Montpetit, *The House of Commons and Its Members* Budgetary Entitlements.

28   CONFLICT OF INTEREST CODE FOR MEMBERS OF THE HOUSE OF COMMONS (Canada)

This "second—home" allowance amounts to about $40,000 a year. But the rules are loose enough that British MPs have been filing claims for mortgage relief, accessories, furniture and repairs on their second homes.

Some British MPs have also indulged in the practice of switching their second residences so that their allowance can be applied to another property.

Canadian MPs say they don't have access to this "second home" gravy train. All MPs are allocated up to $25,000 annually to cover their living expenses —— mostly accommodation and food —— while in Ottawa, or on official trips elsewhere in the country.

MPs are allowed to assign a portion of the living expense allocation to home costs —— about $750 a month —— if they have a secondary residence, a house or a condominium, in the capital.

Each MP works out his or her own living arrangement in Ottawa. Abbotsford MP Fast pays just under $1,000 a month for an apartment. Vancouver—Quadra's Murray stays in hotel rooms which, she says, average between $120—130 a night"[29].

Life in Ottawa was not all work. Occasionally a few MPs and Senators would have dinner together at a local restaurant to unwind and guess what – talk politics! Another diversion for me was the Liberal Caucus hockey team which played 3—4 games a year. We had matches with the Conservative Caucus hockey team, and teams from the Department of National Defense and the Assembly of First Nations, and others. On occasion, games were organized to raise funds for charities.

Our Liberal Caucus had some hockey talent – in particular Senator Frank Mahovlich, and MPs Ken Dryden, and Gary Carr – all former professional hockey players. Unfortunately, while we welcomed Dan McTeague and Denis Coderre as our goaltenders, and Hector Cloutier as our spiritual leader, the former pros were noticeably absent from our Caucus team – with one notable exception involving Frank Mahovlich.

Hec Cloutier organized a game for our team as part of the annual winter carnival in his riding in Pembroke, Ontario. The match featured our Caucus team versus a team comprised of local mayors, reeves, police and fire chiefs. The game was well publicized and as we arrived at the arena in our van, groups of hockey fans were spread out awaiting our arrival. The bubble was burst—that they were there to meet our team—when they

---

29   Ward, Doug Transparency breeds accountability : Canada's House Of Commons staff won't stand for MP—expenses shenanigans like those in Britain, Vancouver Sun, June 13, 2009

immediately followed Frank Mahovlich, not the rest of the team, as we exited the van! Frank went on to tie the game 6—6, as we fed him the puck with five minutes to play – a perfect political solution and a result which added to the ambiance of the post—game reception.

Given that fact that I was an Ontario MP who was born and raised in Montreal, Québec and could speak some French, I approached the Chair of the Québec Caucus soon after my first election in 1996. I offered my services in the fight to keep Canada whole and indivisible. I was told to support the Katimavik program, notwithstanding my desire to contribute at a more intense level than this. Katimavik is a program that brings together young Francophone and Anglophone Canadians and organizes them into teams to assist with community projects across Canada. The program consists of many groups of youths, aged 17 to 21, drawn from all across Canada who travel together to three different locations across the country over nine months. They are chosen to represent the demographics of Canada. They perform roughly 35—40 hours a week of volunteering in the local community and complete a learning program that focuses on Canada's official languages, protecting the environment, leadership, cultural diversity and leading a healthy lifestyle. One of those locations is situated in French Canada. It is a very worthwhile initiative because it exposes young Canadians to each other and helps to build respect and tolerance, but I was nonetheless surprised that my Québec Caucus colleagues viewed this as the number one priority for my engagement in the fight for national unity. I approached the spiritual head of Katimavik, Senator Jacques Hébert, and he suggested we meet in Montreal sometime for lunch to discuss how I might help. Senator Hébert had achieved national prominence when he staged a hunger strike outside Prime Minister Brian Mulroney's office in 1986 when funding for Katimavik was cut. He was totally committed to this program which became very clear to me when we met at a Chinese restaurant in Montreal, L'Orchidée Chine on Peel Street, some weeks later. We sat at the same table where Senator Hébert and former Prime Minister Pierre Elliot Trudeau used to meet to discuss politics years earlier. The Senator told me that the Liberal government, under the leadership of Jean Chrétien, had restored some of the Katimavik funding, but not sufficiently to allow the program to operate effectively and efficiently. Senator Hébert asked me if I would fight for more money for this program. I told him I would. He told me that the program needed voices of support from outside of Québec – especially from Ontario—to make the appeal for more funding more tenable and convincing.

Following this meeting, I began to organize support for Katimavik within the Ontario caucus and I began to speak out about the value of the program as a nation—building block inside and outside of Caucus.

The next federal budget brought back much of the lost funding for Katimavik to the great surprise and delight of the Senator, myself and others. The role, if any, that the interventions from the Ontario Caucus made will never be known, but Senator Hébert was convinced that they had made the difference. He and I became good friends and confidents after that. He came to my riding during at least one election campaign, and perhaps two, and met with young people in my riding to tell them the story about how I had fought for Canada's youth.

A few years later, he called me and asked me if I would like to go to Cairo, Egypt to attend the opening ceremonies, and cut a ribbon, for a Canadian company based in Montreal that was opening an office in Cairo. He was unable to attend, I was told, and he wished to give me the opportunity to do so if I was available. The company would fly me to Cairo business class, put me up in a 4—5 star hotel for 3—4 days and all I had to do was attend the opening ceremony and read a speech prepared by staff at Canada's embassy in Cairo. It sounded too good to be true. The company meant nothing to me and I knew that I was not being put into a conflict—of—interest situation. I would need to disclose the trip to the House of Commons Clerk for all to see, but I had no hesitation to do this. I checked my schedule and with some adjustments I would be able to make the trip. I thanked the Senator and contacted the company representative. All the travel arrangements were made and the speech written when I received a call from our Whip asking me to stay in Ottawa in lieu of Cairo because I was needed for an unexpected vote! That was the end of my introduction to Egypt. Fortunately, Senator Hébert and the company representatives were very understanding which helped to ease my huge disappointment. It was a sad moment for me when the Senator passed away in December 2007. He was a great Canadian.

In a further ironic twist, in 2009, following a UN anti—corruption meeting in Doha, Qatar, my wife and I traveled to Cairo to begin a nine day tour of Egypt, including a cruise down the Nile River, only to discover that we had the wrong entry visas—and so visiting Egypt was not possible that time either. I began to think that touring Egypt was not in the cards for me! Fortunately we were able to visit Egypt one year later, with the correct visas, and just prior to the anti-Mubarak uprising.

Samosas, halal lamb, beef jerky, pasta and Naan bread

There are many people in Canada who don't know who their MP is, and they can't imagine how their MP could help them or be of any use. I gave up asking Canadians in random encounters the name of their MP to avoid the blank stares that often followed. In Etobicoke North, and in many other areas across Canada, there are many demands placed on local MPs. I think part of the explanation is cultural. In some countries, more reliance is placed on elected officials than in others. New immigrants also face many unique challenges and look to their MP for help. My former riding of Etobicoke North has a very diverse population with people from all over the world who have chosen Etobicoke North to be their home. In 2006, new immigrants comprised 64% of the total population of 107,110. Visible minorities made up 71% of the population—with South Asians representing the largest component at close to 50%.

Knowing your MP can be advantageous on occasion. I recall an incident which occurred during the 1997 general election. Joanne, a friend, called in a panic asking for my help. She was traveling to Cape Town to attend a conference and deliver a paper, and on the way there she stopped over in Zurich, Switzerland for a brief interlude. While shopping one day in Zurich, she was pick—pocketed and lost her purse which contained her passport, all her identification papers, all her money and just about everything else. She had a connecting flight to Cape Town in just two days time and desperately needed a new passport. I told her she would need to make her way quickly to the Embassy of Canada to Switzerland and Liechtenstein located in Berne, Switzerland. I undertook to contact the Embassy in advance and alert them about Joanne's predicament. As luck would have it, I had recently met our Ambassador to Switzerland and Liechtenstein at meetings at the Parliamentary Assembly of the Council of Europe in Strasbourg, France. Réjean Frenette and I had been early morning jogging partners in Strasbourg and there was no hesitation from him when I called and provided him with a positive reference for Joanne. Needless to say, Joanne's passport was ready and waiting for her when she presented herself at the Embassy in Berne and she went merrily on her way to Cape Town in time to give her speech.

That incident taught me something else – it is always a good idea to alert the local Canadian Embassy when you are traveling abroad – especially in countries that are not politically stable.

One should never by shy to raise an issue with your MP. The last three years my wife and I lived in Etobicoke before we retired to Victoria, B.C. were spent in a high rise condo tower. It didn't take long for the local condo residents to figure out that their very own MP was living amongst them. Many animated discussions followed in the gym locker room and sauna, in the pool and in the bar—b—que area. One day Dr. Ron Groshow, a fine retired gentleman who is very active in local volunteer work in Toronto, approached me in the gym locker in a state of frustration. He had just returned from renewing his Canadian passport. He asked me why passports in Canada were so expensive, and why the renewal term for Canadian passports was five years, not ten years as is the case in some other countries. I told him that these were good questions and, not having previously investigated these matters myself, I would take the matter up with the Minister of Foreign Affairs, Hon Peter McKay, PC, the minister responsible for Passport Canada, and advise him of the outcome of my enquiries. The Minister responded to me quickly and indicated that, beginning in 2011, Canadian passports will be higher—security electronic passports that will be valid for ten years instead of the current five. When I relayed this information to Ron Groshaw, he was thrilled with the news. Another happy customer!

My constituency office was a very busy place dealing with the problems of constituents on a continuous basis. One staff member in my office was devoted exclusively to immigration matters and was typically swamped with work. Issues ranged from assisting constituents with the processing of their landed immigrant or citizenship application; to intervening at times with failed visitor visa applications for relatives attempting to attend a wedding or funeral in Toronto. We dealt with many other immigration problems as well – cases of identity problems with misspelling of names; failed refugee claims; integration into the workforce issues; difficult sponsorship applications, etc.

In addition to immigration matters, I assisted constituents with tax problems with the Canada Revenue Agency; those denied disability pensions; insolvent students with student loans; delays or problems with passport applications; companies seeking government loans or grants; Employment Insurance (EI) and training eligibility problems; not—for— profit agencies in the riding seeking federal funding; and many other unique problems.

In addition to helping constituents solve problems, I also organized messages and certificates to be sent from the Queen, the Governor General, the Prime Minister, Ontario's Premier, Toronto's Mayor and myself to celebrate various milestones like birthdays, anniversaries, and the like. I also presented awards to various constituents from time—to—time for special accomplishments or contributions to the community. I attended weddings, funerals, Remembrance Day services and Legion events, and I even had an annual fair that I attended to judge a baking contest!

When in Toronto, there were many events to attend and many speaking engagements. The large Punjabi community in Etobicoke North invited me to a continuous string of meetings and events, and I grew to love and respect these very political people. With some effort, commitment and sincerity these people were my biggest supporters and I was very glad to have them on my side. Local gurdwaras (Sikh Temples), especially the Sikh Cultural Centre, became my second home and I developed a taste for Indian food – especially samosas, naan bread and pekora.

I was able to assist the Sikh Cultural Centre when they moved to a much larger property in the riding by supporting them in their efforts to attract well known and admired priests and musicians (ragis) from India for events at the gurdwara. These guests from India helped the local Sikh community raise money to help finance their big move.

The BAPS Shri Swaminarayan Mandir, a Hindu temple, (www. toronto.baps.org) was built in my riding at a cost of some $40 million and officially opened with great fanfare on July 22nd, 2007. The temple was constructed by two thousand builders, engineers and advisors who were required to follow ancient Hindu rules and techniques handed down from generation to generation in India using Turkish limestone and Italian marble. I was able to assist with the large and complicated program to bring these artisans from India – and ensure they returned after the work was done. This was accomplished without any glitches.

Etobicoke North is home to the third largest Muslim population in Canada. Many Friday afternoons and weekends were also spent at the mosque of the International Muslim Organization (IMO) in my riding and over time we developed a respectful understanding of each other.

The leadership and members of the congregation of this mosque always struck me as moderate and peace—loving. After the terrible tragedy of 9/11, I visited the local mosques to assure people that all Muslims were not stereotyped as terrorists or members of Al—Qaeda. I also asked the Imams and other mosque leaders to speak out strongly against the violent tactics used by terrorists which involved the killing and maiming of innocent bystanders. Some years later, in 2005, following the terror attacks in London, UK, a large number of Muslim imams in Canada signed a joint declaration denouncing these terrorist tactics. Prime Minister Paul Martin wisely decided to meet with these imams to thank them for speaking out publically the way they had, and to begin a long overdue dialogue with the Muslim community in Canada. The meeting with these Muslim leaders was held in a hotel in my riding. I was invited together with two other Liberal Muslim colleagues in Canada's Parliament. The Prime Minister attracted much media attention to this event and he used it well to publically thank the imams and congratulate them for this courageous move. Once the media left we had a productive discussion which led, amongst other things, to an outreach program that I was very much involved with. Before the election in 2006, representatives from the RCMP, CSIS and the Canada Border Services Agency and I had organized and attended meetings in a number of cities in Canada where we had full and frank discussions with Muslim—Canadians on a range of issues. Some changes were made to our federal policies and procedures to accommodate the legitimate concerns of this community. More of this outreach should be done as we strive to understand each other better, and to be more sensitive to our respective cultures and religions.

As a rookie MP I found it strange to mix religion and politics in a Sikh gurdwara or Muslim temple but over time I got used to the idea. Sikhs especially expected me, when speaking at their temple or at the seniors' club, to discuss what was happening in Ottawa and I was not to be shy making partisan attacks on other political parties. I initially found this difficult as I stood next to the Sikh holy book, the Sri Guru Granth Sahib

Ji, and my speech followed priests and raggis who read and sang from this scripture.

I have many Sikh friends who helped me understand Sikh culture and traditions – including my colleague in the House of Commons – Hon. Gurbax Singh Malhi, PC who canvassed with me and helped put up campaign signs in the windows of local shopkeepers during my first and second election campaigns. One time, at a regular Saturday meeting of the South Asian Seniors celebrating a Sikh Guru, in my remarks I mixed up the names of the Gurus to the horror of those assembled. I confused the tenth Guru, Guru Gobind Singh Ji, with Guru Har Gobind Ji, the sixth Sikh Guru. A deathly silence followed. Fortunately Gurbax came to my rescue in a very discreet way and a problem was averted.

Not all Asians were welcome in Etobicoke North and here I refer to the Asian longhorned beetle which landed in Vaughan, just north of my riding around 2003. Most of the trees attacked by this beetle in Ontario were maples - a species in abundance in a very fine residential area in my riding called Thistletown. Unfortunately, some of these beetles were unknowingly transported into Thistletown and were detected by the Canadian Food Inspection Agency. Amongst other things, The Canadian Food Inspection Agency (CFIA) is responsible for development of forest policies that prevent the introduction and spread of regulated pests into Canada. Although the beetles were detected in a small grove of large trees, the CFIA warned me that all the trees in this charming residential area might have to come down. The CFIA professionals indicated that such action might be necessary to halt the spread of the beetle into adjacent parks and recreation areas, which would result in the complete destruction of these important civic assets. I realized that this would be devastating news for the residents of the area so I asked representatives from the CFIA to come to my riding and present their findings, and the range of available options, at a town hall meeting that I convened in Etobicoke North. I will remember that meeting for a long time as it was probably the toughest political challenge I had faced in a while. Residents of Thistletown were loudly unanimous in their opposition to any form of harvesting program in their area. The crowd was raucous and not very friendly. Rob Ford, a local city councilor - who went on to become the Mayor of Toronto, hopefully not on the basis of his performance at this town hall meeting, arrived at the meeting and added more fuel to the fire with unresearched and mindless comments and objections.

After the townhall meeting my staff and I regrouped and we decided that I should meet with my friend and colleague, Bob Speller, the then Minister of Agriculture and Agri-Food, at the time, so that I could present to him a plan B to deal with the beetles. The CFIA reports, and is responsible to, the Minister of Agriculture and Agri-Food. My proposal was for the CFIA to cut down the small grove of 3-4 trees that had been infested with the Asian long horned beetle and examine them to determine if the beetles had exited the trees. If they were still inside the trees, there was the possibility that this was the only small area in the riding that was affected. More comprehensive surveys of all of the other trees could then be conducted and if there was no more evidence of beetle infestation, there would be no need to harvest all of the trees in this area. Surveys could be done continuously over time to ensure that the spread had been halted. The Minister agreed. We waited patiently for the results of the tests on the selected trees. I was able to convince the local residents that losing 3-4 trees was a much better proposition that losing all the trees in this attractive residential area. Good news from the CFIA finally arrived. The beetles had not exited the target trees and therefore it was very possible that these were the only trees affected. Further surveys over the following months and years produced no evidence of more beetles. We were ecstatic. I announced another town hall meeting at which the CFIA and I presented the results. This was a much happier town hall meeting than the first one! Perseverance and patience had paid off again.

In addition to the large Sikh and Muslim populations in my riding, there was an interesting mix of Italian—Canadians, Somali—Canadians, Ghanaian— Canadians, Nigerian—Canadians, groups from the Balkans especially Croatia, Jamaican—Canadians and individuals from Eastern Europe. I worked closely with all of these groups, especially the Somali community who had come to Canada in the early 1990s as refugees to flee the bloody civil war there. Many of them came to Dixon Road in my Etobicoke riding and took up residence in the many high rise apartments there. Knowing they would never return to Somalia, I focused my efforts on assisting them in becoming landed residents and then citizens of Canada. Huge obstacles were in the way of this, and our immigration ministers, my colleagues, got to know me and my Somali friends very well 'up close and personal' as we fought for what was right for them and right for Canada.

As an MP I often spoke out about the need to maintain the credibility of Canada's immigration and refugee system. There are those who come to Canada and claim refugee status, when in fact they do not fit the criteria.

Rather, they are economic refugees seeking a better life in Canada. This is fair enough but they should be required to apply in the normal way and not be allowed to jump the queue. My argument centered on the need for refugee claims to be processed more expeditiously so that legitimate refugees could find a home in Canada, and bogus claimants denied entry into Canada. Unfortunately refugee claims often take 4-7 years to process - an injustice to legitimate refugees and an affront to Canada's generous refugee program.

There are individuals who try and escape prosecution in their home country by running to Canada as I discussed in The Poverty of Corrupt Nations -

"Some corrupt officials will arrive in Canada and claim refugee status on the grounds that their safety is at risk and that they would be subjected to torture and perhaps death if they returned to their home country. They might claim the reason for this is the political views they hold and perhaps political activism (always non-violent) against the new ruling party. They are not likely to indicate to Canadian (or any other country's) immigration officers that they had to quickly leave their home country because of their corrupt activities. Fortunately Canada's immigration officers and the Immigration and Refugee Board (IRB) often are not convinced in cases like this and immigration is denied—but I am sure that many slip between the cracks. In fact, some years ago law enforcement officers described to me how many of the so-called Russian mafia had regrettably ended up in Toronto and were engaged in a variety of criminal activities. The violence and brutality that these criminal elements wreaked on each other and on innocent victims was a stark reminder to me of the need to keep people like this out of Canada. I was told also how Russian criminals in Canada make Italian mob types look like Boy Scouts. For the Russians, breaking knees and bones constitutes unnecessary delay. Getting in the way of the Russian mafia often is terminal.

Perhaps my cynicism shows, but I have read through a number of IRB appeal transcripts during the last dozen years. I recall my experience of attending a meeting of the Immigration and Refugee Appeal Board in Toronto. To be a "fly on the wall," I needed the approval of the IRB, and the lawyers on both sides, which in this case was the lawyer for the appellant arguing against his client's deportation, and the federal government lawyer, arguing the opposite.

The individual in question (let's call him Mr. Ahmed) was from Ethiopia. His lawyer argued that he should be granted refugee status because returning to Ethiopia would put him at grave risk including the possibility of execution by government authorities in that country. On the other hand, the federal government lawyer argued that, notwithstanding such risk, he should be deported anyway because he himself, prior to leaving Ethiopia, had been involved in tyrannical acts and crimes against humanity in his home country. Under Canadian, and perhaps international law, such a case can be made and a refugee claim quashed in circumstances like this.

Mr. Ahmed acknowledged that during the rule of known dictator and despot Halie Selassie, he had worked in a political, non-violent way (according to him) as part of a group intent on the overthrow of President Selassie. He was a banker at that time. When President Selassie was finally replaced by Mengistu, Mr. Ahmed (according to his submissions) was asked to join President Mengistu's secret police—in the accounting department. Mengistu was overthrown himself in 1991. Suddenly all those involved with Mengistu's regime, which turned out to be even more violent, brutal, and corrupt than the Selassie regime, had worked in the accounting department. Federal government lawyers successfully challenged his credibility and he was deported back to Ethiopia—to an uncertain fate...."[30]

Building stronger business relationships between Ghana in Africa and Canada became an important part of my work as well. Canada and Ghana have a long history of cooperation and friendship. Ghanaian—Canadians strike me as very entrepreneurial, genuine and friendly. Their President at the time, John Kufour, impressed me with his commitment to good governance and to his fight against corruption. I helped the local Ghanaian—Canadian community create the Canada—Ghana Business Council and we pursued a number of initiatives – some more successful than others. In 2001 I had the honour to meet with President Kufour one—on—one at Rideau Hall when he visited Canada. Every year I would attend the Ghanaian Independence celebration at a local community hall. This was a fascinating event as people strolled into the room dressed in their finest colourful tribal costumes—at 10 p.m. even though the start time was advertised for 7 p.m.!

Over the years in Etobicoke, my wife and I experienced many six or seven course Italian dinners at weddings or at banquets hosted by the St. Andrew's Senior's Italian Group. These were always fun, albeit somewhat repetitive after the first three banquets.

I recall an invitation I received to the wedding reception of a Somali—Canadian friend and constituent. Reading the invitation I would have appeared at the reception at the indicated time of 7 p.m., but given some

---

30   Cullen, Roy, The Poverty of Corrupt Nations, Blue Butterfly Book Publishing Inc., Toronto, 2008, page 68

other experiences, I decided to check with some other Somali—Canadian friends about the timing.

"There is no need to show up before 10 p.m.", I was told emphatically.

Later, on the day of the event, I made my entry into the local banquet hall at 10:15 pm, only to find that I was the first to arrive! After waiting unsuccessfully until shortly after midnight for the bride and bridegroom to arrive, and in anticipation of a very busy work schedule the next day, I left the premises after downing a 7 UP and drooling over the covered food which could not be tasted until the wedding party arrived. I was told later that, in accordance with Somali custom, after the ceremony in the Muslim mosque, the couple retired to a local hotel to 'consummate' their marriage and presumably were having so much fun that they forgot about the reception which followed!

Most of my interactions with constituents were positive experiences – with some exceptions. One constituent, a Canadian citizen I will refer to as CG and who I shall never forget, came to me complaining that the wife he had sponsored had arrived from Eastern Europe and, after a few weeks, had deserted him. He claimed that she never had any intention to remain with him but had married him solely as a way to gain entry to Canada – a marriage of convenience.

Why she left him is not known. It could be that she left him because they were not compatible, or because he was abusive. As Rt. Hon. Pierre Elliot Trudeau said in 1967, 'There's no place for the state in the bedrooms of the nation'.

On July 17th, 2006, I wrote to the then Minister of Citizenship and Immigration, the Honourable Monte Solberg, P.C., M.P. and suggested the following approach to the problem of 'marriages of convenience' —

"………..One possible solution would be to place the sponsored spousal applicants who arrive in Canada on probation, where the applicant must remain with the spouse for a specified period of time. Failure to do so would trigger an investigation and eventually a hearing in front of a panel of individuals appointed by Citizenship and Immigration Canada (C.I.C). The panel would review the facts presented, and would make a determination if this marriage took place for the sole purpose of gaining admission into Canada. If it was determined that there was a marriage of convenience, the applicant would have his/her permanent resident status revoked and removed from Canada.

There would be a number of examples where couples have separated due to an abusive relationship. If this is the case, and the panel has reached this conclusion, then I would propose that the applicant could remain in Canada if he or she desires to do so. I would not wish to see an individual punished because they are involved in an abusive relationship. This would also encourage people to come forward and alert the authorities if they are involved in such a relationship.

Citizenship and Immigration Canada is currently involved in the processing the 'front—end' of immigration applications. Canada's missions posted abroad have been given the responsibility to determine if an applicant is involved in a genuine marriage. The tasks performed by CIC are generally completed once the applicant arrives in Canada and has been granted permanent residence status. I believe it is time for C.I.C. to involve itself in the 'back—end' of processing immigration applications and ensure that the applicants remain with their spouse once in Canada".

Monte Solberg spoke to me in the House one day, and expressed his concern about marriages of convenience, and promised to look into the matter and consider my proposal. After a cabinet shuffle, I followed—up in person with the new Minister, the Hon. Diane Finley, P.C., M.P., to no avail. The problem still exists and no significant changes have been made to policy or legislation to my knowledge to address this growing problem which attacks the credibility of our immigration system.

When CG came to me with his complaint, I did a follow—up with the Minister of Citizenship & Immigration at the time because CG alleged the woman he had sponsored had not been truthful on her immigration application. These claims proved to be impossible to substantiate.

CG, who had been rude and abusive to staff in my constituency office, barged into my Toronto office one day when I was in Ottawa, and overturned book cases and computers before my staff could call the police and have him arrested. He expressed his dissatisfaction with the progress on his complaint, when in fact there was nothing further that could have been done. He was taken away and detained for psychiatric assessment. Through legal counsel in the House of Commons, I was able to obtain a court order forbidding CG from coming within 500 meters of my office, my staff, myself or my wife.

At a meeting with one of the elders from CG's community, I learned that CG was a member of a local gun club and was a competent sharp shooter! Upon learning this, a report went out quickly to the RCMP branch that protects MP's, and to Division 23, the local Toronto Police Services police detachment, and a judge approved a warrant for CG's apartment to be searched. Surprisingly no guns were found. CG's explanation was that he had sent the guns back to his home country, a country exiting from civil war. When the police asked him for the paperwork to substantiate the export of the guns, none was forthcoming. This caused much consternation to my staff and myself because it was then possible and plausible that the guns were in fact hidden somewhere in Etobicoke. This led to the expense of changing the security arrangements in my constituency office with changes to the door entry procedures, and the addition of bullet—proof glass in the exterior windows. This, thankfully, was the worst experience I encountered when trying to help a constituent with a problem. After this one, any other mini—confrontations seemed minor by comparison.

Other colleagues of mine in the House of Commons were similarly affected from time—to—time. I recall a friend of mine, a Toronto area MP, who had to have the fax number at his constituency office changed when a disgruntled voter in his area flooded his office with huge volumes of frivolous faxes each and every day over a protracted period – designed simply to vandalize his office and create problems for him.

From time—to—time one's personal life intersects with the role as MP. I will provide the following three examples—

In 1996 when I first ran for Parliament in the by—election, my wife and I lived in mid—town Toronto, near the Mount Pleasant Cemetery – a long way from Etobicoke North. During the campaign, being up against three candidates from the other mainstream political parties who were born and raised in the riding, I indicated that I planned to move into the riding – which is what I did after my election victory in 1996. There is no requirement to live in the riding you represent, but I preferred to live in the riding – and besides I had promised I would move into Etobicoke North. To digress momentarily – Roy MacLaren was the individual who preceded me and served with distinction for many years as MP in Etobicoke North. Roy lived with his wife Lee and family in Forest Hill throughout his tour of duty in the House of Commons– a very upscale community in Toronto. Roy told me an almost unbelievable story about something that happened to him at an all—candidates meeting during one of the election campaigns he fought. Someone went to the microphone following the speeches from the candidates and posed the following question—

"Mr. MacLaren, why should we support you when you don't even live in this area?" the constituent asked.

Roy carefully considered his options, and decided on the following response –

"Well, sir, if you had a choice and you could live either in Forest Hills or Rexdale (a somewhat pejorative way of describing Etobicoke North), which area would you choose?" Roy offered.

There are few politicians who would venture such an answer – and in this case get away with it!

Returning to my story, for the bulk of my time serving the residents of Etobicoke North in Ottawa, my wife Ethne, and for a while our son Peter, lived in a three level house on a quiet cul—de—sac in the riding. When my father was no longer able, for health reasons, to clear the snow from his property in Montreal, I became the proud owner of a 'kick—ass' Ariens snow blower. When snow conditions were optimal, meaning light, fluffy snow, I would enjoy clearing my walkway and driveway on those rare occasions when I was in Toronto and we had a serious snow fall.

One morning in particular sticks in my memory. Following a large snowfall, I was out early blowing snow in every which direction. Feeling particularly altruistic, and loving the soft, light snow, I decided to clear the walks and driveways of our two immediately adjacent neighbours – one because she was a single, working mother who needed to get to work; and the other in recognition of his age and heart condition.

The snow removal done, and exhilarated by the feeling of accomplishment, I proceeded after breakfast to my constituency office for a typical day of meetings. Mid—morning my staff handed me a bunch of phone messages for me to respond to, and one had the name of an individual who lived across the street from me. I didn't know this individual, but being curious about the reason why a neighbor would phone, I put her message on the top of the pile and rang her number.

"Mr. Cullen", she said, "I am a senior widow who lives on your street and I am marooned in my home because the snow is piled high around me and this is preventing me from exiting my house. Are there any federal government programs available to shovel me out?"

There are certainly some strange federal programs, but removing snow for individual citizens was stretching the imagination!

I immediately connected the dots and concluded that this person had stood at her window that morning, and watched her MP remove the snow from his home and that of his immediate neighbours. I assumed that she was feeling left out! Fortunately I recalled that there was some assistance available from the City of Toronto for stranded seniors and I was able to arrange snow removal for her by calling her City Councilor.

Another incident involved a local real estate agent who got me into a lot of trouble with a constituent. My wife and I have always had an interest in real estate. We have renovated two homes and we are always on the lookout for good value. One Sunday we were exploring a street in my riding that was a cul—de—sac and very quiet. It was Fathers' Day and I was being taken to lunch. We came across a house for sale that looked interesting and placed a call to the real estate agent who was listed on the for sale sign to enquire about the home. The agent provided us with the information we were seeking and then she asked us if we would like to have a tour of the property. We declined on the basis that it was Fathers' Day and a chosen day for family get—togethers. The agent insisted that this would not be a problem and undertook to confirm with the owner of the property and to call us back. This she did, explaining to us that the owners were very happy to have the agent show us the house later that day after lunch. The house had been on the market for over a year and we assumed they were anxious to sell.

We arrived at the home after lunch to be welcomed by the real estate agent who showed us around the property. In so doing, we noticed various family members who had obviously congregated to celebrate the day with their father. Our visit was deliberately kept brief following which we indicated to the agent that while the house was a quality home, we weren't sure it was of interest to us for a variety of reasons. We promised to contact the agent the next day to give us some time to reflect on the situation.

The next morning, after my wife and I had had the opportunity to discuss the matter the previous evening, I called the agent and told her we would not be proceeding with an offer. At my constituency office later that day, I was handed a telephone message slip requesting that I call the owner of the property we had just visited the day before. I thought this unusual as the practice was to work through the real estate agent, but I picked up the phone and called the owner of the house. What followed was a barrage of abuse and acrimony – complaining that I had no real interest in their property and that we had interfered with their family gathering. I explained that indeed we had an interest in their property and that the agent had assured us that viewing the house that day was not a problem. These words fell on deaf ears and he promised that within their family unit there were ten votes that heretofore had always been cast in my favour, but that this would not be the case in the next election! I apologized for any inconvenience we had caused and emphasized that we had been serious buyers and left it at that.

After finishing with this call I placed a call to the real estate agent. She confirmed my suspicion that she had told the owner that I was the local MP. I told her that this was completely unacceptable and that I was not happy at all with this breach of confidentiality. But the damage had been done and I reflected on the fact that if I had been someone other than an MP, the home owner would not have had someone to lash out at. Again, this struck me as a good example of the ramifications of public life and of being in the public eye.

Earlier on in my political career, a number of powerful lessons were learned by me in the lead up to our party's leadership convention in 1990. From 1980 until 1987, when I served as an Assistant Deputy Minister in the British Columbia government, I had to suspend my involvement in partisan political activities, including my previous involvement with the Liberal Party of Canada. As an ADM, the hours were often long and frequently I found myself in my office when the cleaners would arrive. The people doing this work were a Punjabi family working under contract with the BC Buildings Corporation and we would converse and exchange pleasantries when they arrived at the office to do their cleaning. We got to know each other at a certain level and I grew to respect their commitment to hard work and their entrepreneurial spirit. When I left the BC Government in 1987 shortly after Bill Vander Zalm became Premier, I immediately re—engaged myself in local Liberal Party politics.

In 1989 I was supporting Mr. Chrétien's leadership candidacy and was part of a campaign team in Victoria, B.C. working to elect him leader of the Liberal Party of Canada. We had identified two important gurdwaras in the area that were involved in the leadership campaign – one gurdwara supporting Jean Chrétien and the other temple behind Paul Martin's candidacy. I was asked to meet with the leadership of the Temple supporting Paul Martin, with the objective of bringing them over to the side of the Jean Chrétien supporters. Of course, the leaders of Sikh gurdwaras are in a position to influence their congregations, and they are very politically active and astute and they command the respect of their followers. A name and coordinates were given to me and following a call to the Head of the gurdwara, a date and time for our meeting was set. The address was a house on Beach Drive in Victoria – a very 'upscale' area with large homes and beautiful properties.

On the evening of our meeting, I located the beautiful home and when I knocked on the door, I was completely taken by surprise when I was greeted by the Punjabi woman who had been part of the office cleaning team that I had befriended a few years earlier. Inside, her husband and co—worker turned out to be the leader of the gurdwara. We had a good meeting and although they did not commit to Mr. Chrétien at that time, I do recall that we won all of the delegates to the leadership convention. From this episode a few didactic conclusions –

- always be pleasant with people from all walks of life. It is the right thing to do and one never knows where or when one might encounter them under quite different circumstances;
- as the saying goes, never judge a book by its cover. I would not have expected that the cleaning staff at my office would own such a beautiful home; and,
- show some humility and avoid ostentation. The family cleaners, as with most Sikhs, were humble about their origins, their work and their wealth.

When in one's riding, much interaction with one's riding association takes place. The main mission of a riding association is to facilitate the nomination of a candidate, and once that is done, to help the candidate win the election. Some of the key work for the riding association is –

- election campaign fundraising;
- working on election campaigns as key members of the campaign team;
- expanding local Party membership;
- organizing social events in the riding to thank volunteers and raise the profile of the Liberal candidate and/or Liberal MP;
- development of policy resolutions;
- sending delegates to Party conventions to vote on policies, amend Party by—laws, elect Party leaders, etc.; and,
- advising the MP of developing local issues, problems and opportunities.

I was very fortunate to have Diarmuid Horgan as the President of the Etobicoke North Federal Riding Association for all but two years of my tenure as MP. Diarmuid was also the longest serving Liberal riding association President in Ontario, and someone I often turned to for sage and wise advice.

For many years, my riding association organized a highly successful annual bar—b—que picnic which attracted up to seven hundred local participants. The afternoon on the lawns of the Humber College Arboretum, with access to a huge marquis tent, proved to be a very big winner as people enjoyed hot dogs, hamburgers, vegetarian pizza and samosas, ice cream, followed by door prizes, a few speeches and background music from a young and talented Humber College jazz band. Hopefully they came to meet me, and not just for the free food and prizes.

For many years the Etobicoke North Federal Liberal Riding Association organized and ran an annual Christmas Levy where tea, coffee, and juices were accompanied by sandwiches, veggie dips, samosas (of course!), and cakes and cookies. This was a great way of sharing the holiday spirit with many people in my constituency. For years this was held at the St. Philip's Church Hall and it was a well attended and popular event.

Visitors to my constituency office included from time-to-time those who asked me to intervene for groups of individuals who were the subject of persecution abroad. These included representatives from-

- Falun Gong in China
- Assyrians in Iraq
- Ahmadiyya Muslims in Pakistan and Africa
- Bahá'í Faith in Iran
- People's Mujahedin of Iran (PMOI)

In this work I was very careful not to embroil myself in conflicts abroad that I knew little about, but if I was convinced of the merit of the case, I might write a note to the Minister of Foreign Affairs and ask him/her to investigate the claims and report back to me. One matter on which I refused to take a position was the claim that the Armenian population of the Ottoman Empire was deliberately and systematically destroyed during and just after World War I - referred to as the Armenian genocide. I told those who wanted the Canadian parliament to condemn the genocide that I was an MP, not an historian; and I questioned why the House of Commons should be engaged in this debate of historical events that occurred years ago and miles away. What would be gained by our parliament asserting that there was or was not a genocide?

All in all, constituency work is very varied and often interesting and challenging.

Representing Canada Abroad –
If it's Tuesday it must be Strasbourg

One of the favourite pastimes of Canadians is to poke fun at parliamentary 'boondoggle junkets' when they hear about Canadian MPs traveling abroad on various missions. What people don't often appreciate is Canada's leadership role in the world and how this translates into the need for elected officials in this country to be represented on the world stage. In my judgment, it is not sufficient for government ministers to be Canada's voice abroad. Parliamentarians of all political stripes need to be engaged on global issues and speak out from a Canadian perspective.

Early on as an MP I decided to focus my attention on Europe, so I joined the Canada—Europe Parliamentary Association. There are many other such associations that are available for membership by MPs and Senators including organizations like the Canada—USA Parliamentary Association, the Canada—NATO Parliamentary Association, the Canada—Africa Parliamentary Association, the Canada— Japan Parliamentary Association, and the Commonwealth Parliamentary Association. These associations select Canadian parliamentarians to attend meetings held from time—to—time, in Canada or abroad, to discuss and debate a variety of issues. Resolutions are typically passed at these meetings and reports are presented to relevant ministers of governments. For example, the Parliamentary Assembly of the Council of Europe meets about four times a year in Strasbourg, France. The Canada—Europe Parliamentary Association selects a bi—partisan group, usually 4—5 strong, of Canadian MPs and Senators who attend these meetings and participate in the debates in the Parliamentary Assembly and in the various committees. Resolutions are passed and reported to the Committee of Ministers. The Committee of Ministers is the Council of Europe's decision—making body. It comprises the Foreign Affairs Ministers of all the member states, or their permanent diplomatic representatives in Strasbourg.

Speaking at the Parliamentary Assembly of the
Council of Europe in Strasbourg, France

Canada has observer status, as does Mexico and Israel, in the Parliamentary Assembly of the Council of Europe, and is able to speak in the Assembly Hall and at committee meetings. I had the honour to be the first Canadian MP to speak in the Parliamentary Assembly, in the Hemicycle – on the topic of economic crimes in Eastern Europe.

As delegates to the Parliamentary Assembly of the Council of Europe, we Canadians often fought battles in Strasbourg to protect Canadian interests. For example, during the debates in Europe about the contentious seal hunt in Canada, we fought hard to ensure that European parliamentarians had information, not misinformation, about this industry that is so vitally important for many Atlantic Canadians. On one occasion, as delegates we facilitated a presentation by officials from Fisheries & Oceans Canada to the members of the relevant parliamentary committee at the Council of Europe.

Working with the late Hon. Charles Caccia, P.C., in October 1998 Senator Gerry Grafstein and I hosted, under the auspices of the Canada—Europe Parliamentary Association, a seminar in Ottawa entitled —*Beyond NAFTA to a Canada—Europe Transatlantic Marketplace*. We enjoyed a strong attendance from European Parliamentarians and left the seminar agreeing that we should work towards a Canada—Europe free trade agreement. I was inspired to promote this agenda as a result of many discussions I had had with my predecessor in Etobicoke North, Hon. Roy MacLaren, P.C., who has tirelessly advanced the idea that we need to diversify our trade and enhance our trade and investment with Europe. Some 70%—80% of Canada's exports flow to the United States. We have failed to commercially capitalize as a nation on our cultural and historical roots with Europe. Roy MacLaren's efforts over the years are finally beginning to pay dividends as a Canada/European Union free trade agreement appears to be close at hand.

My work with the Canada—Europe Parliamentary Association took me on a number of occasions to Strasbourg, France– a city I grew to love for its beauty and charm. Sitting outdoors in a patio restaurant sipping a café aux lait and staring up at the magnificent looming cathedral in the city's central square are moments, however brief, that will linger with me for a long time. The canal that weaves its way through and around Strasbourg, and the mix of German and French influences on the local cuisine both add to the appeal of Strasbourg.

When attending meetings in Europe as part of a Canada—Europe Parliamentary Association delegation, which typically consisted of four or five MPs/Senators and two staff, our economy class travel was arranged by the staff at the Association. We were often able to get upgrades to business class if we had the required certificates. We were reimbursed for accommodation, meals, taxis and other incidentals while on travel status by means of a per diem allowance. The per diem allowances were usually realistic but not overly generous which is appropriate when coming from the public purse. I recall a few meals that easily surpassed the per diem allowance and I was required to pay the excess out of my own pocket – in particular one meal with Senator Frank Mahovlich and his engaging wife Marie at *Au Crocodile* restaurant in Strasbourg; and on another occasion again with Frank and Marie at *La Perle du Lac* in Geneva, Switzerland.

Mexico, like Canada, has observer status at the Parliamentary Assembly of the Council of Europe and given our North American and NAFTA connections, we would always meet with the Mexican delegates over lunch in a restaurant housed at the Council of Europe precinct. We would cover a range of topics at these lunches and then engage in some idle chatter. I recall at one of these sessions I asked the Mexicans how they viewed Hugo Chávez Frías, the President of Venezuela. They all smiled, leaving me with the impression that they thought more highly of other world leaders. Being diplomatic, however, they avoided any negative comment but one Diputado (Mexican Congressman) told us a story of an invitation he had once received to attend a small dinner party at the Presidential Palace of Mr. Chávez. As the group of fifteen attendees took their places at the table, it became clear that, in addition to the President's place at the head of the table, one other chair was missing a participant. When the President finally entered the room and took his place, he welcomed those in attendance, pointed to the empty chair, and told those assembled that that chair was reserved for Simón Bolívar. This surprised the group given that, although Mr. Bolívar was much loved and respected for the key role he had played in Latin America's successful struggle for independence from Spain, he had died in 1830!

During my years as an MP, I spoke out often at international meetings on the dire need to fight global corruption and money laundering – activities that are robbing citizens around the world of the ability to move out of the ranks on the poor. In 2005 I had the opportunity to introduce two resolutions at the Parliamentary Assembly of the Organization for Security and Cooperation in Europe (OSCE). Both resolutions were adopted by the Assembly as a whole. One dealt with global corruption and the other with money laundering.

The policy of the Parliamentary Assembly of the OSCE is that Committee Chairs or raporteurs are obligated to complete their work on a study or project they have started, notwithstanding their status as an elected parliamentarian. This rule is in place principally because MPs from time—to—time lose elections and are booted out of office, but the work of the Parliamentary Assembly must continue. Following the 2004 general election in Canada, I had the opportunity to attend the July 2004 meeting of the Parliamentary Assembly of the OSCE (PAOSCE) in Edinburgh, Scotland. At this session more than 300 parliamentarians from 52 OSCE participating States adopted the Edinburgh Declaration focusing on the political, economic and human rights aspects of the central theme of the Session: 'Co—operation and Partnership: Coping with new Security Threats.' One member of our Canadian delegation was New Democratic Party MP Swend Robinson who, in his capacity as Acting Chair of the Parliamentary Assembly Committee on Human Rights and Democracy, and General Committee Rapporteur, was presenting a report on the role of the OSCE in the fight against terrorism following work he had completed on this project on behalf of the committee. Svend's participation proved to be controversial, because in April, 2004, just prior to June 28, 2004 federal election, he had been found guilty of stealing an expensive piece of jewelry at an auction. He resigned from the House of Commons in June 2004 but he felt obligated to fulfill his responsibilities and complete his work with the Parliamentary Assembly of the OSCE. I supported his decision and said so publically.

Another equally controversial, but largely unnoticed, event occurred in 2004 in Edinburgh. A Conservative MP, who will remain nameless but let's call him JK, arrived in Edinburgh with one of his assistants and tried to register his staff member as a participant at the OSCE meetings. Parliamentarians all understand that this is not permitted and they simply do not bring support staff to these meetings. This did not deter JK. After attending the Scottish cultural welcoming event hosted by the OSCE and the Scottish Parliament on the first evening of the Parliamentary Assembly, where JK enjoyed Scottish dancers and a scrumptious pig roast dinner, he and his assistant disappeared. JK failed to attend any of the meetings – notwithstanding the underwriting of his travel costs by Canada's Parliament and the Canadian taxpayer.

When I was reached by a CTV reporter at my hotel in Edinburgh, I was asked about Svend Robinson's attendance at the meetings. I responded that however uncomfortable the situation was, he was simply following PAOSCE policy and following through on certain personal undertakings that he had made to the organization.

I took the opportunity to tell the reporter about the JK story which heretofore she had no inkling. When she asked me if I would go on—air with my comments on the Svend Robinson story I responded that I would – on one condition. That condition was that during this on air interview I would also want to comment on the JK fiasco. I never heard back from CTV. That was not the story they were working on nor interested in.

I had the opportunity also to advance the anti—corruption agenda at meetings of the Commonwealth Parliamentary Association as well as the Canada—NATO Parliamentary Assembly. In addition, in September

2003 I was a guest speaker at a Conference on Parliamentary Oversight of the Sphere of Security, Defense and National Economy in Kiev, Ukraine. My topic was *Money Laundering and Corruption as New Threats to National Security*. While in Kiev, I took the opportunity to meet with our Ambassador, Andrew Robinson, who briefed me on the situation in Ukraine. He also kindly treated me to two extra tickets he had to a ballet recital at Kiev's famous National Academic Theatre of Opera and Ballet. I shared the tickets, and an unforgettable experience, with an Hungarian MP who was also participating in the NATO meetings. The only similar event that trumped this one was when my wife and I were treated by the Russian State Duma to a performance of the ballet Don Quixote at the Bolshoi Ballet when I was in Moscow working with members of the Finance Committee of the Russian Parliament.

For Canadian MPs and Senators, these opportunities are important and shouldn't be downplayed. Parliamentarians represent Canadians abroad in other ways – in addition to work with Parliamentary Assemblies. Since 2000, I have been an active member of the Global Organization of Parliamentarians Against Corruption (GOPAC) which has taken me to meetings and conferences around the world – working with parliamentarians from many other countries on strategies and actions needed in the fight against corruption and money laundering.

Interesting twists can also occur when on parliamentary delegations. I recall a bi—partisan delegation I led to London, England some years ago where our focus was the work of the European Bank for Reconstruction and Development (EBRD). The delegation consisted of five Canadian parliamentarians—two senators, and one member each from the Bloc Quebecois and the NDP and me. Over our 3—4 days of meetings in London we had one free evening. We all went our separate ways – I took in a play – and we agreed to meet in the pub in the hotel close to the last call around 10 p.m. for a night cap. When I arrived after the play, the two senators were involved in an active discussion, and apparently in doing so in their private, but loud, conversation they had inadvertently insulted an American patron of the pub by making what he perceived to be an anti—American remark. The U.S. resident of England, who was quite drunk, tried to start a fight with the offending senator. I had to intervene to stop the nonsense and fortunately a bad situation was averted. I had envisioned a headline in the next day's newspapers – *Canadian Parliamentarians embroiled in fisticuffs in local pub!* As leader of the delegation this motivated me strongly to interject myself into the situation!

There are other occasions when MP's and senators are required to travel abroad. From time—to—time Standing Committees of the House of Commons visit other countries when they are studying a selected topic and information is required from other jurisdictions on how these governments and parliaments have approached the same problem or subject matter.

Backbenchers often accompany ministers of the government to international meetings. As a government member, MPs are often chosen as a way to reward their hard work and team play. Opposition MP's are usually invited to accompany ministers so that MPs are 'paired' in the House of Commons and important votes not lost!

During my time as an MP, I had the opportunity to travel with Hon. Bill Graham, P.C. on two occasions – when he was Minister of Foreign Affairs and later when he served as Minister of Defence. I have the greatest admiration for Bill, and over the years we became good friends. We travelled together to India, Sri Lanka and finally to Thailand where Bill and I attended a meeting of the Asia—Pacific Economic Cooperation (APEC) Group. The trip to Moscow when Bill was Defence Minister was also very interesting especially the meeting and long lunch with Russia's engaging Minister of Defence, Sergei Ivanov—a senior Russian Federation Minister who had at one time been touted to succeed President Putin. Apart from his habit of chain smoking cigarettes throughout our meetings and meals, we enjoyed our wide ranging and engaging discussion with him. The trip with Bill Graham in 2003 to Sri Lanka had one unusual twist. Given the civil war that was in progress in Sri Lanka at that time, pitting the Sinhalese Government against the Liberation Tigers of Tamil Eelam (LTTE) we had insisted that in addition to meetings in Colombo, Sri Lanka's capital, we would meet with members of the Tamil community on their 'turf" so that we could hear both sides of the story. A trip to Jaffna was organized – a city in the north of Sri Lanka that was populated by the Tamils, but which, at that time, was occupied by some 30,000 Sinhalese troops.

With Paul Martin & Bill Graham - two of my key mentors

After arriving in Jaffna and a briefing by the Sinhalese military commanders there, we went on a tour of the area and then met for lunch with a small group of Tamil leaders. Following a lively and informative discussion there, we went across the street where a reception with a broader group of local Tamils had been organized. While the reception was in progress, I became aware of a commotion that was emanating from the front door to the community hall where the reception was being held. As one can imagine, security was very tight at these and other events in Jaffna. Three individuals were attempting to join the reception but they were not on the list of invitees under the control of security guards. As the noise grew louder, I managed to get the attention of one of Bill Graham's assistants who went to investigate what was happening. He reported to me that three Tamil constituents of Bill Graham who lived in Toronto, knowing that the Minister would be in Jaffna on the appointed date, had traveled by plane and car all the way from Toronto to Jaffna so that they could meet up with him in their country of birth. Not surprisingly, Bill quickly interceded in this matter and the three visitors were granted entry to the reception. Can you imagine the negative political fallout in

Canada if they had made such an effort and had still failed to meet with their MP?

Over the years I had other opportunities to travel with minsters. Once I accompanied Hon. Pierre Pettigrew, P.C., to Geneva in 2005 when he was Minister of Foreign Affairs to attend a United Nations conference on disarmament. In addition to Pierre delivering a speech on disarmament in the Palais des Nations, we had a number of bilateral meetings with the foreign ministers of other countries. One such meeting was with the Minister of Foreign Affairs for Ecuador. Around that time Pierre was being touted as the next Secretary General of the Organization of American States. The meeting was conducted almost entirely in Spanish – presumably Pierre was trying to impress the Minister from Ecuador with his fluency in Spanish. With my fluency in Spanish limited to ola and cervesa por favour, participation in the discussion was impossible. Although this was mildly irritating, and most unusual, I decided not to 'rain on his parade'. Following our meeting I did comment to him about the fact that the dialogue was in Spanish. He reacted with a comment along these lines –

"Well, you know, the media always speak about my apartment in Paris and my long hair, but they never mention that I am trilingual!" Proving once again that politics and large egos are comfortable bedfellows.

Pierre Pettigrew demonstrated this on another occasion – a reception in the garden at the Prime Minister's residence, 24 Sussex Drive, following my swearing—in as parliamentary secretary to Anne McLellan. Over a glass of wine, Anne, my wife and my son were engaging in quiet conversation to celebrate the moment at the cocktail reception when Pierre Pettigrew barged into our conversation, uninvited, and began attacking Anne for not supporting him on some issue at cabinet. I was furious with this behaviour, as was my family.

India beaconed in 2002 when I was asked to participate in a Team Canada trade mission designed to promote more trade and investment between India and Canada. I enthusiastically agreed to participate and because of the large population of Indo-Canadians in my riding, and my interest in seeing trade increase between our two countries, I forwarded the invitation to Canadian businesses from International Trade Canada to my own list of business contacts, some of whom ultimately joined the mission. One individual in particular, a close friend of mine and Canadian business executive, decided to make the trip to India. One evening in Mumbai (Bombay), we decided to venture out to a jazz club after the mix-and-mingle trade mission hospitality function. We agreed to meet in the hotel lobby at 9 pm and proceed to *Not Just Jazz by the Bay* - a local establishment on the outskirts of Mumbai next to the Arabian Sea. I had checked earlier with the hotel concierge who advised that a jazz trio was indeed playing that evening at the club. We jumped in a taxi and made our way to the venue and the doorman confirmed that the jazz concert would begin in ten minutes. Inside, we ordered a drink from a waiter who checked his watch and told us "any minute now." Low and behold, instead of a jazz ensemble, a karioke program began moments later with the full participation of the local patrons who crooned very amateur 50's and 60's rock numbers for the 'enjoyment' of those assembled. Confused and annoyed, I called the maitre d'hotel to our table and complained that we had been told repeatedly that a jazz trio would be playing that evening around this time. "Oh", he replied, "we haven't had jazz artists here for about five years!" We were shocked and puzzled and left shortly afterwards thinking that a name change for the club might be in order, something like - *Used to be Jazz by the Bay*! Later we laughed about the experience, but at the time we were perplexed and angry about the turn of events.

I travelled on one or two occasions with Hon. Anne McLellan, P.C. when she was Minister of Public Safety and Emergency Preparedness. In September 2005 she invited me to join her on a trip to Pakistan for discussions on national security issues, but in the end I unfortunately had to decline because of other pressing matters in my constituency.

While serving as parliamentary secretary to the Rt. Hon. Paul Martin, P.C., when he was Minister of Finance, I had the honour to represent the Minister at a meeting of the Board of Directors of the European Bank for Reconstruction and Development (EBRD) in London, England, and later at meetings of the Organisation for Economic Co—operation and Development (OECD) in Paris to participate in a discussion on the topic of harmful tax competition.

In 2005 I accompanied the Rt. Hon. Paul Martin, P.C. when he led a Team Canada mission to mainland China and Hong Kong. My wife Ethne accompanied me, adding to the overall experience and giving us some time together. When I traveled abroad on government or parliamentary business Ethne often would join me. We would book, and pay for, her airfare, together with the price differential for upgrading the hotel rooms from single to double occupancy. Time permitting, we would add a few days at the end of the parliamentary meetings and do some sightseeing on our own at our own expense. While I was attending meetings during the day, Ethne would reconnoitre the area. We used this information to target what we wanted to see and do on our own. Ethne would usually accompany me to receptions and dinners that were often scheduled after business meetings were completed during the day.

In Beijing we had an interesting experience. As a result of a Cabinet shuffle back in Ottawa, some of my meetings in Beijing were cancelled – resulting, serendipitously, in two days of free time. Hon. David Anderson, P.C. found himself in the same situation in Beijing so we decided to do some sightseeing together. We were convinced by Jean Duval, the Prime Minister's Mandarin translator, to visit a local pet market frequented exclusively by local Beijingers. Jean, who in appearance looked more like a Francophone Canadian than Chinese, had been the mandarin translator for Canada's Prime Ministers going back to the time of Lester B. Pearson. His Mandarin was impeccable as we were to discover. The pets at the market consisted of tropical fish, birds of all description, and crickets – yes crickets! The locals use a listening device to identify the cricket sound of their choice. After purchasing the cricket it is put in a small box and it is carried around in a top pocket and rubbed by its owner to elicit the uplifting cricket sound. This was fascinating in and of itself but the more amazing phenomenon was to witness the expression on the faces of the locals when Jean spoke in Mandarin. They smiled from ear to ear because they had rarely if never heard such perfect Mandarin come from the lips of a white, European—looking male! They gathered around him in amazement and at the end of our visit to the market a small group of some fifteen locals were following us around. Jean, in addition to his Mandarin skills, has a good sense of humour and turn of phrase which kept the group laughing and interacting with Jean for some time.

I discovered later that Jean was the product of a mixed marriage – one parent French speaking, and the other from Turkmenistan.

While in Beijing, a group of us met with representatives of the International Division of the Chinese Communist Party at their office tower in the city. Around this time, a Chinese state-owned enterprise, China Minmetals, was trying to acquire Noranda Inc. - a transaction that I did not favour and had spoken out against. I decided to risk not being politically correct - after all we had traveled some 10,500 kilometres to reach Beijing - and raise the issue of the takeover bid. I told the Party representatives that this purchase of Noranda was quite controversial in Canada. Had the PRC thought of privatizing China Minmetals, I asked. This might provide Canadians with more confidence that the transaction was based on market-based principles, and might improve the chances of approval in Canada, I conjectured. What followed was an informative and useful history lesson by a senior Communist Party official of the role of state-owned enterprises in China - especially the large natural resource companies. These companies over the years had contributed over 60% of state revenues - so there was no way they would be sold off. By the same token, they were not for sale to interested foreign buyers - end of story. By way of contrast, I thought how naïve we are in Canada sometimes, and how we could do a much better job of protecting our strategic assets and our national interests.

On another trip to China in 1999, I traveled with representatives from Humber College, a large and respected institution in my former riding of Etobicoke North, to Beijing to deal with a problem Humber was experiencing with respect to foreign students. Humber was anxious to attract students from China as a way of 'internationalizing' their student body and as a means of enhancing their revenues with foreign student fees. To accomplish this they had entered into a strategic partnership with Ning Bo University, near Shanghai, China for a student exchange program. These objectives were being stymied because of the failure of many of the applying Chinese students to obtain student visas to visit Canada.

When representatives from Humber College first approached me to discuss their problem, and asked me to accompany them to Beijing, I decided first to do some research. What I discovered was that our Government had been experiencing problems with students from China. Many of them were not honouring their student visas and once in Canada were disappearing and escaping the purview of Citizenship & Immigration Canada. I told Humber that, to ensure that our trip to Beijing was productive, we needed to develop a 'business' model for their Chinese student program that would respond to the issues facing our Canadian embassy in Beijing. Having worked in British Columbia years earlier as a senior bureaucrat, I understood the power of elected officials, but I realized also that without a solid policy/program rationale, proposals for action stood little chance for success.

Humber College responded very positively and quickly and came back to me with a 'business model' for their student program which featured the following three key elements –

1. Chinese students would be required to successfully complete course work at Ningbo University following their studies at Humber College—before their Business Diploma was granted to them;

2. all monies assembled by each student (usually in the vicinity of Can $ 30,000) would be held by Humber College in trust for them and drawn down exclusively for student tuition, books, other study material, and living expenses; and,

3. students, upon returning to China following their stay in Canada as students, would be required to photocopy the returning stamp in their passport and submit same to the Canadian Embassy as proof of their return.

I complimented the Humber College officials for understanding the problem and addressing it in their proposal. I asked them to summarize their 'model' in two—three pages and then we would be off to Beijing to sell the program, which we did. Because of this work we were able to convince Canada's Beijing Embassy officials that this approach was sound. The Embassy began to approve student visas for Chinese students bound for Humber and we experienced no visa failures for many years as a result; i.e. all of the students successfully returned to China following their studies in Canada. I was very proud of this accomplishment and used it as an internal example of how to 'get things done' in the sometimes rarefied air of our national government.

Interestingly, a few days before my departure on this visit to China, On May 7th, 1999 during the Kosovo War, NATO forces bombed and destroyed the People's Republic of China embassy in Belgrade, Yugoslavia. It was widely known that Canada's Air Force was very much involved in this operation. Given this fact, I decided to contact the Department of Foreign Affairs (DFAIT) and ask them if it was wise for me to travel to China at that time especially since the Chinese government was outraged and understandably very angry about this attack on their embassy which had resulted in three fatalities and three injuries. I had also been told that students at Ning Bo University, where I would be visiting, had staged a protest march from the university to the city hall in response to the bombing. The official in DFAIT told me he would review the matter and contact me the next day. When he called me he advised that it was OK for me to travel to China but I was offered the following advice –

- keep a low profile;
- stay away from rallies and demonstrations; and,
- if asked about the bombing incident, apologize on behalf of the federal Government and indicate that the matter was being reviewed by the Government to determine what occurred and what changes needed to be made.

I decided to proceed to Ning Bo but wondered if the advice I had received from DFAIT was much more than obvious, and whether it had been worth waiting for! How was a 6' 2" while male to keep a low profile? In fact, while I was there, I was stopped numerous times by locals who wanted to be photographed with me simply because I was tall and white.

There are two competing theories about what happened on that day in Belgrade. Was the bombing directed to the wrong target as the USA and NATO originally claimed; or, was the speculation that the Chinese Embassy had housed a communications center to gather intelligence on NATO weapons and equipment on behalf of the Serbs, closer to the truth ? We may never know, but I am more inclined to believe the latter explanation. In any event, I safely went to and returned from China without incident.

Traveling to various locations around the world as a representative of Canada's Parliament or the Federal Government provided me with many opportunities to meet, interact, and converse in small groups with exceptional people – like former US Secretary of Defence, Robert McNamara; the former President of Taiwan, Chen Shui—bian; the former President of Ghana, John Kufour, the former Prime Minister of Sri Lanka, Ranil Wickremesinghe, the former Russian Deputy Prime Minister and Defence Minister Sergei Ivanov, former US Attorney—General John Ashcroft, the first United States Secretary of Homeland Security, Tom Ridge, and many others.

Another highlight was meeting Diana Krall, the Canadian jazz musician, in Taipei, Taiwan when she was there on tour in August 2002. As delegation leader, I worked with the Executive Director of the Canadian Trade Office in Taipei (CTOT), together with the Taipei Economic & Cultural Office (TECO) in Ottawa, to organize our one week information gathering tour of Taiwan. These one week visits to Taiwan are fully paid for by the Taiwanese government through TECO and as such are considered Sponsored Travel and reported by Canadian MPs to the Clerk of the House of Commons. The Clerk maintains a registry of such travel which is open to all, including the media, to see. The Taiwanese leaders view these events as an opportunity to present their side of the ongoing dispute with the People Republic of China to Canadian Parliamentarians, but to some these sponsored travel opportunities are blatant attempts to buy influence. I must say, I was clear with TECO that I supported the long standing 'One China' stance of our federal government, but that I was interested in understanding better the history and background of China/Taiwan relationships by interacting first hand with the Taiwanese and Chinese peoples. Some years later I did support Taiwan's application for observer status in the World Health Organization (WHO) because I believe Taiwan can make a large and important contribution to this organization. Finally, in May 2009, after twelve failed attempts to join the United Nations' World Health Organization as an observer, Taiwan was invited to take part in the WHO's World Health Assembly in Geneva under the name "Chinese Taipei"'

Let's get back to Dianna Krall. Leading up to our tour of Taiwan, I discovered in discussion with the Executive Director of our Trade Office that Diana Krall was performing in a concert in Taipei during the week of our visit. I asked if we had any 'free' nights in Taiwan and was told there was one evening with no events planned. I was, and remain, a huge fan of Diana Krall.

"If the delegates are interested in attending the concert at their own expense, could you arrange tickets for the group", I asked.

"Certainly we could do that" was the reply.

I canvassed the six—seven delegates and most, if not all, of them wanted tickets to the concert. I conveyed this to the Exec Director and he undertook to purchase the tickets and I committed to paying him when we arrived.

"Would it be possible to meet Diana Krall backstage at the concert", I enquired.

"We would like to meet her and, who knows, she might think it was 'cool' to socialize with Canadian parliamentarians so far away from home", I asserted.

"That could be a tall order, but I will see what we can do" was the response.

"Great. Let's speak again in a few days to see where we are with this", I added.

Sure enough, CTOT organized a backstage reception and invited thirty members of the local business community and local politicians, and also representatives from Taiwan's music industry to the event. BINGO!

After the sold out concert and after numerous standing ovations from the audience, we began our walk down the centre isle to the stage area. As I was doing so, someone from CTOT approached to warn me that Diana was very tired and may not stay too long at the reception. Ugh, I thought to myself.

One of the delegates on our tour was the Conservative MP from Nanaimo, Reed Elley. I had asked Reed to say a few words after the introductions, since Diana hailed from Nanaimo, and present her with a small gift from the Parliament of Canada which I gave to him before the show.

Diana arrived backstage and I introduced myself and the other members of the delegation. After a few other introductions I gave the floor to Reed. He spoke very well, I thought, and touched on the fight that Diana's mother had experienced with cancer of the breast, and how her mother had crusaded against breast cancer while she fought her own battle. Knowing that Diana and her mother had been very close and that her mother has passed away only months earlier, I glanced over at Diana and tears were rolling down her cheeks. She headed for the wing of the stage. O my goodness, I thought, what now?

In a few moments, Diana was back giving Reed a big hug. One of my poorest delegation decisions ever, I thought! Diana stayed at the reception for about forty minutes and the evening was a huge success. I still have Diana's autographed photo framed and hanging on my wall and my CD collection grows.

We have all had problems with lost or misplaced luggage but my worst experience occurred in July 2000 when I attended the 9th annual session of The Organization for Security and Co—operation in Europe (OSCE) Parliamentary Assembly, in Bucharest, Romania. On the way I had arranged to meet with the Canada—Ireland Business Council in Dublin to learn more about the economic success story in Ireland following their accession into the EU in 1973, and after they had significantly reduced income taxes and made Ireland very attractive to investors. My wife Ethne accompanied me on this trip, as she sometimes did. She would pay for her own air travel and for any additional costs for accommodation and meals, but it was a great way for us to spend some time together and to jointly experience other countries of the world. We arrived in Dublin just prior to Canada Day, July 1st and we had made arrangements to stay with Ambassador Ron Irwin and his wife Margaret at the Canadian Embassy residence just outside of Dublin. Ron had been a colleague of mine in the Liberal caucus and had served with distinction as the Member of Parliament for Sault Ste. Marie and as Minister of Indian Affairs and Northern Development. The Canadian residence, called Strathmore, at that time was located on a sprawling nine acre property and for fifty years had been the official residence of the Canadian Ambassador in Ireland. It has been described as one of Dublin's most important residences. The property is located next door to a stately home owned by Irish rock star Bono.

This historic property was sold in 2008 against the objections of many former Canadian ambassadors in a property swap in exchange for a luxury home in an upscale downtown Dublin neighbourhood. The deal also included a cash payment of $4.8 million to the Canadian government, the negotiated difference in value between the two properties. Canada had purchased the property in 1957 for $54,000, but when it was sold its value was estimated at €17 million.

Ambassador Irwin had organized a Canada Day celebration on the lawns of Strathmore and, at a time when federal government budgets were strained, Ron had hustled Canadian businesses operating in Ireland and raised sufficient funds to host a gala reception for seven hundred people! The Irish military donated a marquis tent which housed the Guinness and Molson Canadian keg operations, and a variety of hot foods. The lawns of Strathmore absorbed the crowd easily and in fact the nine hundred people who had been invited would have rounded out the event had it not been for a characteristic light drizzle that failed to mar the occasion. Irish fiddlers added to the occasion and at the appropriate time the Ambassador asked me to say a few words and bring greetings from Canada, our government, and Prime Minister Jean Chrétien, which we did. To add some levity, I cited a jingle that had become much popularized in Canada at the time of my visit to Dublin. It was a Molson Canadian *I am Canadian* 'rant' which I recited fortunately to large doses of laughter —

Hey, I'm not a lumberjack, or a fur trader....
I don't live in an igloo or eat blubber, or own a dogsled....
and I don't know Jimmy, Sally or Suzy from Canada,
although I'm certain they're really really nice.

I have a Prime Minister, not a president.
I speak English and French, not American.
And I pronounce it 'about', not 'a boot'.

I can proudly sew my country's flag on my backpack.
I believe in peace keeping, not policing,
diversity, not assimilation,
and that the beaver is a truly proud and noble animal.
A toque is a hat, a chesterfield is a couch,
and it is pronounced 'zed' not 'zee', 'zed' !!!!

Canada is the second largest landmass!
The first nation of hockey!
and the best part of North America

My name is Joe!!
And I am Canadian!!!

What struck me at this July 1st celebration was the reaction in the crowd as Canada's national anthem was played. As I glanced around at the faces of those assembled, the number with moist eyes I noticed was quite astounding. It demonstrated that even though these Canadians were in Ireland for a variety of reasons, and by choice, their ties to their native land were still very strong.

We said goodbye to Ron and Marg, and to the staff at the Embassy residence, thanked them for their kind hospitality, and we flew to London Heathrow on Air Lingus, and then on Lufthansa flights to Frankfurt and to our final destination, Bucharest. My wife and I had checked one bag each in Dublin to interline all the way through to Bucharest. Of course, when we arrived in Bucharest, our bags were noticeably absent. It took Lufthansa five days to locate and deliver our bags to our hotel in Bucharest. Fortunately, with the help of a similarly sized member of the Canadian Embassy staff in Bucharest, and a small clothes shopping spree after day two, we were able to cope and I was able to be suitably dressed for my meetings.

The illusive appointment to Cabinet

Most MPs, if they are truly honest, when they first arrive in Ottawa aspire to be appointed to cabinet. Precisely how Canadian Prime Ministers decide on the make—up of their cabinets is known only to a few, but factors like competency, regional representation, gender and racial balance all come into play. In the general elections of 1993 and 1997, when the Liberal Party of Canada formed majority governments, there was a preponderance of MPs from Ontario, making the competition particularly fierce. In the 1993 general election, my party won 177 seats (out of a total of 295) of which 98 seats were from Ontario (55%). The comparable numbers for the 1997 general election were 155 seats for the Liberal Party (out of a total of 301) of which 101 (65%) were Ontario MPs. In the 2000 general election we won 172 seats, of which 100 (58%) were from Ontario.

I was elected for the first time in a by—election in 1996 and fourteen months later I successfully fought in the 1997 general election and re—entered Parliament as one of the 101 Liberal MPs in Ontario. Certainly these numbers did not work in my favour as a relative rookie, and as Prime Minister Jean Chrétien attempted to form a cabinet that had representation from all provinces and territories with a mix of female ministers women and representatives from visible minorities reflecting Canada's diversity.

Not making it into cabinet was a big disappointment for me from a career perspective, but I was fortunate to have had the opportunity to serve in a variety of interesting and challenging assignments.

As a member of the Prime Minister Jean Chrétien's government, and later under Prime Minister Paul Martin, I served as chair of the House of Commons Standing Committee on Finance, as parliamentary secretary to the minister of finance, as parliamentary secretary to the deputy prime minister and the minister for public safety and emergency preparedness; and as chair of the Ontario Liberal caucus. I also served as Official Opposition critic for natural resources when Bill Graham was our interim leader following the 2006 general election. In 2004 I was sworn in as a member of the Queen's Privy Council for Canada.

I was fortunate to work with Paul Martin and Anne McLellan as their parliamentary secretary during periods of significant change and unique challenges. The minister of finance, given his other responsibilities, does not log many hours in the House of Commons or at Standing Committees of the House or the Senate debating and promoting finance bills. This largely fell to me as parliamentary secretary – a challenge I relished. Interestingly roughly 30%—40% of the Bills that pass through Parliament emanate from the Minister of Finance and Finance Canada, so the workload was quite heavy and intense. During my tenure, we successfully steered the passage of a variety of bills, including formative anti—money laundering legislation - the *Proceeds of Crime (Money Laundering) and Terrorist Financing Act*; massive changes to the *Bank Act* to deal with bank mergers amongst other things; and two *Budget Implementation Acts* to implement a variety of fiscal measures, including the largest income tax reduction package in Canadian history totalling $100 billion. The Department of Finance (Canada) is exposed to the full range of government—wide issues and is a great vantage point into the workings and priorities of government.

Working with Anne McLellan, in her dual roles as Deputy Prime Minister and Minister of Public Safety and Emergency Preparedness, gave me the opportunity to participate in the fine tuning of Canada's anti—terrorism laws; to implement the restructuring of the department to respond to the threat of global terrorism; and to assist in the development of a compensation package for aboriginal Canadians who had been negatively impacted from their stay in residential schools many years ago.

In an ironic twist, Anne McLellan asked me to tackle a problem that had been brewing in the Canada Customs operations of the Canada Border Services Agency. Following 9/11, the Department of Public Safety and Emergency Preparedness Canada (PSEPC) had been formed, together with the Canada Border Services Agency (CBSA), the latter reporting to the Minister responsible for PSEPC, Anne McLellan. The CBSA was comprised of the front—line services of Citizenship & Immigration Canada (CIC), Canada Customs, and the Canadian Food Inspection Agency (CFIA). The goal was, and is, to better integrate these programs and services at our borders for greater efficiency and enhanced national security.

In the mid 1980's as part of our government's deficit reduction exercise, the services provided by Canada Customs had been frozen at a point in time and 'grandfathered' moving forward. This meant that any new services from that point onward would be provided on a cost recovery basis only. This policy worked for a while, but over time a variety of anomalies emerged. For example, new courier companies were unable to obtain competitive services at airports because these new services provided by the CBSA had to be paid for whereas their competition received the same services for free. This hardly made for a level playing field. Likewise, new ports, like the one in Prince Rupert, B.C., would normally have had to pay for customs clearance services – unlike the Port Of Vancouver, their competition, which paid nothing for these same services.

Anne McLellan, knowing about my private members' bill on user fees (C—212) asked me to sort this out. We had begun the process of defining services into 'core' and 'non—core', rather than 'grandfathered' versus 'cost recovered', when the 2006 election, which our Party lost, was called.

I couldn't help being amused, however, when at the start of this project, I was briefed on the customs fees situation and my Bill C—212 was cited on the PowerPoint™ presentation as a significant obstacle to a speedy changes to the CBSA user fees because of the Parliamentary review process and information requirements!

My friend, and former Liberal colleague in the House of Commons, Barry Campbell describes very well the anxious moments when the Prime Minister is forming his/her Cabinet —

"1993. I sat by the phone waiting for "the call." Days went by. Journalists wrote, and friends and my team told me that I'd be in Cabinet, that he couldn't pass me over. Like all government MPs, I did the calculations: regional balance, gender, friendships, experience, competence, etc. "Maybe a few rookies will squeak in," someone said. "Let me make a call," another offered. "You can't appeal to the Boss directly. He'd take a dim view of that, but let me see what I can do." The Boss probably received 176 "indirect" calls.

Veterans who had weathered the indignity of Opposition waited in silence, while "star candidates" grew apoplectic as reality sank in. All of us were legends in our own minds; few of us got the call. I watched the swearing—in of Cabinet alone, feeling, suddenly, that I wasn't really part of what I was supposed to be a part of. I had some idea of what a Cabinet minister did but no clue what it meant to be a backbencher. "It's for a short time," I assured myself. "There were lots of worthy candidates," I explained to those who asked. I was guessing. One thing was clear: as I wasn't in Cabinet, the Privy Council Office would not send over seasoned pros to get me up and running. I was on my own. I set off for Ottawa"[31].

Barry describes the huge disappointment when the reality sinks in that you are not making it into Cabinet —

"It's not clear which is psychologically worse: getting bounced from Cabinet or being passed over for a position. Not being considered one of the stars is deeply embarrassing and hard to explain to family, friends, and supporters. Grown men and women, accomplished and respected in their fields before coming to Ottawa, are reduced to nervous, insecure children when the rumours start flying about a Cabinet shuffle. I got passed over, and I'm not sure I could have swallowed additional humiliations........

Six years on, I found myself flying to Ottawa on the day Prime Minister Martin was putting the final touches on his Cabinet. Travelling with me were hopeful MPs, confident they would get the call. I remembered the feeling. As I left Ottawa late that afternoon, I was joined by MPs who were not "in" this time. They were upset. I remembered that feeling, too. "Were you in Ottawa providing grief counseling?" one asked me. Another vowed revenge. The disgruntled and disaffected enter a political reverse world: they come to Ottawa to be a force for good, and, consumed by hurt, embarrassment, and panic, they turn to revenge"[32].

I thought my best chance to make it into Cabinet was when Paul Martin formed his first government in December, 2003. But it was not to be. I was offered a role as parliamentary secretary, but in my mood of extreme disappointment, I declined. I will never understand why I was by—passed, nor will my friend and former colleague, Maurizio Bevilacqua be able to explain his rejection I am sure. It was hinted to me at the time that this appointment as parliamentary secretary was a 'stepping stone' for bigger things to come with the next Cabinet, but I was a non—believer at that point.

Following the 2004 election, I was left out of cabinet again and was appointed parliamentary secretary to Hon. Anne McLellan, P.C., Deputy

---

31   Campbell, Barry; The Walrus, *Politics as Unusual: Darkness Visible*, April 2008

32   Campbell, Barry; The Walrus, Politics as Unusual: *Sanity Found*, May 2008, page 77

Prime Minister and Minister of Public Safety and Emergency Preparedness – a demanding and interesting job that I thoroughly enjoyed.

While I understood the challenges of forming a cabinet, and trying to keep everyone happy, what I didn't appreciate were queue jumpers – like Belinda Stronach when, on May 17, 2005, she crossed the floor from the Conservative Party and joined the Liberal Party to become Minister of Human Resources and Skills Development. Martin claimed Stronach's move was due to concerns over the direction the Conservative Party was taking, while others accused Stronach of political opportunism. Here was someone who had run for the leadership of the Conservative Party just one year earlier in 2004! Scott Brison had crossed the floor to our Party in 2003, but it was only after he successfully ran in the 2004 election campaign as a Liberal Party candidate that he made it into Cabinet.

Stepping forward for a moment, after the 2006 election I was courted by some very senior people in the Conservative Party Caucus to cross the floor; but I could never have looked myself in the mirror knowing I had betrayed my political party of choice for close to twenty years for the promise of a chauffeur, a larger office, more fame (perhaps infamy) and more staff.

Earlier, a number of experienced colleagues had told me, perhaps in a sympathy vote because I had not been appointed to Cabinet, that as Paul Martin's Parliamentary Secretary I was privy to information that some junior ministers would not have access to. Indeed the breadth of coverage of the finance department is very broad. I recall at my first meeting with senior department officials at which time I was briefed on the issues they were addressing, I was told about the challenges in 2001 that Canadian Airlines International was facing. When I asked why Finance Canada was following this matter, and not exclusively Transport Canada, I was told that eventually most problems ended up in the lap of the Minister of Finance and his officials. And this proved to be true in my experience.

After being sworn—in in 2004 as a member of the Queen's Privy Council of Canada, I had the opportunity to attend a number of Cabinet meetings and see first—hand how they operated. On one occasion, I made a presentation to the Operations Committee of Cabinet at which time I outlined our parliamentary strategy for obtaining parliamentary approval of the budgetary estimates for the gun registry.

Interestingly, after being sworn in as a Member of the Queen's Privy Council of Canada in 2004, I took on the label of the Honourable Roy Cullen, P.C., M.P. A number of calls came into my constituency office –

``When and why did Mr. Cullen switch over to the Progressive Conservative Party?`` they asked. Of course, they thought the designation of P.C. following my name meant that I had jumped ship!

Politics is a blood sport

Winning a federal election is a two part process. The first task, unless one wishes to run as an independent, is to be named as a party's candidate in a federal riding by securing the nomination either by election or by acclamation. The second part is to run in a federal by—election or general election and win more votes than any of the other candidates. Too often individuals with political ambitions forget the first phase – only to fail and make the second phase redundant.

The best political advice I ever received was from Hon. David Anderson, P.C., when campaigning with him in Victoria in the general elections of 1979 and 1980 (book ends of the short—lived Joe Clark government). When asked how to prepare myself if I ever had the urge to seek a seat in the House of Commons, he told me I needed to 'pay my dues' at the riding association level – and he was right. In 1996, when Hon. Roy MacLaren, P.C., then Canada's Minister for International Trade, was named High Commissioner to Great Britain, it was my service as volunteer treasurer to the Etobicoke North Federal Riding Association from 1991 to 1996 that paved the way for my victory at the party nomination meeting that was held in February of that year. I was up against three other contenders, two of whom were high profile individuals who had both run, unsuccessfully, as Liberal Party candidates in the previous Ontario provincial election. Unlike me, they had not 'paid their dues' at the federal grass roots level in Etobicoke North. I won on the second ballot at the nomination meeting with the support of the riding president and the majority of the executive committee.

The nomination process was an eye opener for me when a couple of key individuals who had promised their support for me turned up at the nomination meeting sporting lapel buttons in support of another candidate. I was almost ill with disgust but still managed to confront one person who provided some lame excuse for switching their support. It was a good introduction to the world of 'in the trench' politics at its worst, and it helped me prepare for the years ahead. There were a number of back stabbing incidents later in my political career that were targeted at me – in some cases by my own colleagues. It was an aspect of political life that I came reluctantly to accept as a reality; but a phenomenon that I never ceased to find abhorrent. I was not alone in this.

Let me provide a few examples of politics as a blood sport.

For the first ten years on my service as an MP I was very fortunate to have a positive and constructive working relationship with my riding association – the Etobicoke North Federal Liberal Riding Association. We never had any problems or disagreements. When there were contentious issues – we worked them out. All that changed in the lead up to the 2006 Liberal Party Leadership Convention to replace Paul Martin. Initially, I supported my friend and colleague from Vaughan, the Hon. Maurizio Bevilacqua. He and I had worked closely together when he chaired the House of Commons Standing Committee on Finance and we had developed a healthy respect for each other. We had also become good friends and so for a variety of reasons I wanted to support his run for the leadership of our party. I thought his chances were slim given the profile of the competition, and as his policy chair I advocated some riskier policy positions so that he could differentiate himself from the rest of the pack and move forward that way.

In a surprise move during the leadership campaign, Maurizio withdrew from the race for reasons that I do not fully understand to this day. Presumably he concluded that his chances for victory were slim (certainly our polling was telling us this) and the leadership campaign was costing him a lot of money. At the time of his decision he called me on the telephone to inform me of his decision and to tell me that he was throwing his support behind Bob Rae. I thought he and Bob were strange bedfellows considering Maurizio's reputation as a 'right of centre' politician – and Bob's previous membership in the leftist New Democratic Party – but I respected his decision. I like Bob Rae and I respect the man but my concern that his political baggage from his term as Premier of Ontario was too much to overcome. It was, and is, my belief, that Ontario voters would not forgive him for some of the policies he introduced when he was Premier of Ontario from October 1990 to June 1995. Ontario was fertile ground for our party and I was convinced the voters of Ontario would take it out on our party if Bob was our leader.

When Maurizio made his decision public, I was at my cousin Suzanne's cottage near Huntsville in the Muskoka, north of Toronto. As a supporter of Maurizio, my cell phone never stopped ringing with calls from the other candidates seeking my support in the transition – even in the canoe while fishing! In the end, I decided to support Michael Ignatieff. Senator David Smith, a respected and seasoned politician, had introduced me to Michael some months previously and I was impressed with Michael's credentials and with his 'royal jelly'. At the time of our meeting, I asked him how he would deal with the criticisms that would follow his candidacy about the fact that he had lived outside of Canada for thirty or so years. Michael responded honestly and candidly to my question and he impressed me with his candor and sincerity.

Some in the Sikh—Canadian community in my riding came to a different conclusion about the leadership race. Many of them decided to support another leadership contender - let's call him S.B. – someone who, for a variety of reasons, I could not back. There were many IOU's outstanding between S.B. and the South Asian community, and I understood this. We had our discussions and in a democratic fashion we agreed to disagree on our choice of candidate and resigned ourselves to signing up more memberships than the other group.

At the delegation selection meeting, where individuals were selected to attend the leadership convention, the Sikh—Canadian group, led by two individuals who had been staunch supporters of mine, managed to sign up more memberships than the Michael Ignatieff supporters in Etobicoke North. People (Sikhs—many who were not fully aware of the nature and objective of the meeting) were transported to the delegate selection meeting in bus loads. They were successful in electing nine committed delegates for S.B., while Michael Ignatieff was relegated to three.

Sometime after the leadership convention in Montreal in 2006, and Stéphane Dion being declared our leader, we were required to hold an Annual General Meeting (AGM) of the riding association. With the benefit of hindsight, we should have postponed this meeting but we proceeded as planned, never for one minute thinking that the S.B. supporters in my riding would try to take over the Association. However, that is exactly what happened. Two Sikh Canadians who had supported me from 1996 until 2006 turned out to be the ring leaders of the coup, much to my dismay and disappointment. I subsequently tried to turn this around without success, leaving a bad taste in my mouth for the last two years of my service in the House of Commons. There were no practical consequences arising from these events, just a feeling of disharmony and a loss in team morale. Our interim Liberal Party Leader, Bill Graham, confirmed me as the candidate in Etobicoke North for the 2006 election, so the political ambitions of the coup leaders went unfulfilled. When I announced in 2008 that I would not be running in the upcoming election, Stéphane Dion, on my recommendation, named a very talented individual, Dr. Kirsty Duncan, to be the Liberal Party candidate in the 2008 general election, which she subsequently won. Kirsty is doing a great job as an MP, and serving her constituents and her country well. She was victorious again in the 2011 general election.

S.B. had a history of causing trouble for colleagues in Etobicoke North. In 1988 he actively worked against the nomination of Roy MacLaren who had lost the 1984 election in the Brian Mulroney sweep. Although the 1988 nomination was designed to be a fairly contested and open event, it takes a special breed of person to fight against a former colleague in caucus and in the House of Commons. During Mr. Chrétien's mandate, my nomination was secured in 1997, 2000, and 2004 as were all sitting Liberal MPs, as a result of the Prime Minister using his authority as Leader of the Liberal Party of Canada to approve candidates for upcoming elections. Leading up to Paul Martin's first election campaign in 2004, nominations were opened up but in my case my candidacy was uncontested. In 2006 Prime Minister Martin guaranteed the nomination of all sitting MPs. The argument for guaranteeing the nominations of sitting MPs has merit inasmuch as MPs can then focus on their responsibilities in Ottawa and on their constituency work, and not be distracted by troubles with riding association memberships often the result of overly ambitious and not loyal political operatives.

As an MP, I had another needle in my side that caused me some anguish. An individual, let's call him Mr. X, had been a loyal supporter and active within the Etobicoke North Federal Association. When I threw my support to Paul Martin to replace Jean Chrétien, I asked Mr. X to take on the role of Membership Secretary in the Association. Prior to this appointment, Mr. X and I had a frank discussion of his mission, as I saw it, and he gladly accepted this. His goal was to sign up new members who were loyal to Paul Martin so that we could obtain the votes for all of the delegates at the delegate selection meeting for the upcoming leadership convention in November, 2003. At that time, Mr. X was a keen supporter of Paul Martin so he readily agreed to this game plan.

Leading up to the convention, however, Mr. X changed his mind and decided to sign up members who supported a range of the party leadership candidates. I confronted him on this point but he would not budge – notwithstanding our earlier agreement. A few weeks later, I called him on the telephone and asked him to take on the role of Director Without Portfolio within the Association – and relinquish his responsibilities as Membership Secretary. He was not happy with this and from that day forward he took great delight in trying to make life difficult for me. His main initiative was to run against me, as an independent candidate, in two general elections. He never was a threat but he created some havoc at the all candidates meetings during the campaigns, and he tried to sabotage my campaign by covering up my signs and lifting my brochures – to the point where I reported him to the police and to Elections Canada.

One of the dumber things I did as an MP was to attend a meeting in 2001 at the Regal Constellation Hotel, in my riding in Etobicoke North with a large group of Paul Martin strategists and MPs. At the time the meeting was called, there was speculation that Paul Martin would be leaving the Cabinet because of some difficulties with Prime Minister Chrétien, including the fact that Mr. Chrétien was giving no indication of stepping down at some point to pave the way for Paul Martin to lead our Party and the Government. At that time I was Parliamentary Secretary to Paul Martin and I was concerned that he might be losing patience with his bid for the leadership. The meeting was called by a group of Paul Martin strategists, people like David Herle and Terrie O'Leary, without my knowledge, and the choice of a venue in my riding caught me completely by surprise.

I made a decision to attend the meeting because I was Paul Martin's Parliamentary Secretary; because I supported Paul Martin's bid to become our leader; and, because the meeting was being held in my riding. I never viewed the meeting as a coup d'état, which is how it was later reported in the press. Again, someone had leaked the fact that this meeting was to take place. Can you imagine an act more Machiavellian or devious than that? It is quite clear that Mr. Chrétien stayed on as Prime Minister longer than he might have otherwise. He and his wife Aline were furious because they saw the meeting as a political betrayal. Aline Chrétien encouraged the Prime Minister to stay on and fight – if for no other reason than to spite the alleged conspirators.

Once the dust settled, I asked for a meeting with the Prime Minister. At the meeting I apologized for my participation and argued that much more had been made of the meeting than what had actually transpired, but the damage was done.

Although the Parliament of Canada is a highly charged partisan environment, the vast majority of MPs and senators do their very best to do what is right for Canadians. Differences come mainly in the choice of priorities and how different political parties view the role of government. There is no denying, however, that political weaknesses are exploited in the quest to remain in power, or the desire to form a government. In all political parties there are those who are highly partisan and ideological. Most MPs, however, are focused on the issues of the day and the policies and programs needed to improve the quality of life for Canadians. We differ mostly on how to get there.

Through GOPAC, I became good friends with former Conservative MP John Williams and a very good working relationship with Joe Comartin of the NDP. Participating in all—party parliamentary delegations is a good way to get to know colleagues in the House of all political stripes. For me, morning visits to the gym atop the Confederation Building was a good way to meet opposition members in a more relaxed setting and talk about something other than politics.

I recall one such morning in the gym, when my cell phone rang as I was changing in the locker room. Conservative MP and Cabinet Minister at the time, Stockwell Day, had a locker close to mine and had just returned from his daily jog. A personal friend of mine had called inviting me to an Atlantic salmon fly fishing lodge in Labrador, as a change of pace from our annual visit to the Eagle River to fish for speckled trout.

"David, this is great", I asserted. "What are the dates", I asked. "July 22nd to July 29th", he replied.

I was shocked and disappointed to suddenly realize that this week overlapped with my 25th wedding anniversary and I, unbeknownst to my wife, had already booked us into a resort hotel in the Muskowka north of Toronto for a few days to celebrate the occasion.

"Are any other dates available? ", I asked as I described my dilemma to Dave.

"That is the only week available, but not a problem. I understand completely. We will try next year." he said.

I apologized and ended the call.

"Stockwell, you won't believe what just happened to me." I said to Stockwell Day as he undid the laces on his running shoes.

"Roy, I couldn't help but overhear your conversation, and you know what, I think you made the right decision!" My wife Ethne couldn't have agreed more and told me so when later I related the story to her.

Machiavellian moments are not restricted to political activities. They can also develop during one's parliamentary work. I recall a series of events that occurred when I was opposition critic for natural resources—events that convinced me that there is, in fact, justice in this world. I should indicate at the outset that I do not consider myself a vindictive person. On the other hand I have a good memory, and the patience to tuck things away in the recesses of my mind for another day. On a visit to Washington, DC with Gary Lunn, the Minister of Natural Resources, we were met at the hotel near Capitol Hill by the then Assistant Deputy Minister (ADM) of Energy Policy for the Department of Natural Resources Canada (NRCan) – let's call him HG. I knew HG in my previous capacity as parliamentary secretary to the Minister of Finance when he served as an assistant deputy minister in that department before being transferred to NRCan. Following a short briefing that HG took the Minister and me through, we continued our discussion over a drink in the hotel bar. At one point in our discussion, HG made some very flattering comments to Minister Lunn, and some subtle but not so flattering references to the Government of Paul Martin. I bit my tongue but was furious. If the ADM wanted to suck up to the Minister, that was fine I suppose; but to do this in my presence was over the top in my judgment.

My chance to even the score came about during hearings of the Standing Committee on Natural Resources months later when we were reviewing the environmental and economic issues associated with the oil sands in Alberta. HG was asked to appear as a witness in his capacity of Assistant Deputy Minister, Energy Policy. During his presentation he essentially asserted that the forces of the market economy would address the many environmental issues associated with the oil sands – i.e. CO_2 production, water recycling, etc. I was astounded by this. Although I have great faith in markets, it was beyond me what incentives corporate Canada would have to reduce greenhouse gas production, or to recycle all of the water used in the extraction of bitumen, absent a regulatory regime or fiscal instruments that demanded or encouraged such action. I challenged HG on his thesis. He stuck to his theory.

At the next meeting of the Standing Committee, the Minister of Natural Resources, Gary Lunn attended our meeting as a key witness. After the minister's presentation, I told him that on the previous day his assistant deputy minister, energy policy, had made the claim that market forces would deal with all of the environmental challenges created as a result of the development of the oil sands. I asked the minister if he agreed with this policy direction and if what HG had presented was in fact government policy. To Minister Lunn's credit, and to my delight, he responded that these assertions by HG were absolutely <u>not</u> the policy of the government. Touché! I rest my case.

In 2008 I decided I would not run in the upcoming election. In my judgment 12½ years in the House of Commons, and five election campaigns, constituted a 'good run' and it was time to move on to a new chapter of my life. Some of my supporters couldn't understand why I wouldn't run again for the sixth time because, in their view, another victory was assured. I thanked them for this vote of confidence and I believed also that I could win the seat again for our party, but my decision not to seek re—election was motivated by other factors. At sixty—three years of age, I believed it was time to retire, or semi—retire, and spend more time with my wife, other family and friends, and focus on new challenges and opportunities.

My friend and former Liberal colleague in the House of Commons, Barry Campbell expressed it so well –

"Some people took my departure as proof "it isn't worth it." Not so. I did my time, made a small contribution, and got out alive. "You have only served five years," others said, suggesting that to be effective you need to spend a lifetime in politics, which is probably the worst thing a politician could do. In fact, Canada would be well served if people moved in and out of politics. There is a huge gap in understanding between the public and private sectors that could be significantly narrowed if more good people moved from one to the other and back again. Unfortunately, there is no real process for reintegrating ex—politicians into the private sector, and if defeated they are considered damaged goods. Also, politics pays poorly compared to many private sector jobs, and, sadly, this keeps good people away".[33]

I am often asked how I became involved in politics and what led to my running for a seat in the House of Commons. Interestingly, until I reached the age of 35, I was quite apolitical. Having qualified as a

---

33   Campbell, Barry; The Walrus, Politics as Unusual: *Sanity Found*, May 2008, page 77

Chartered Accountant in 1972, my focus was on 'crunching numbers' and conducting audits. A good friend of mine, Rick Cannings, convinced me to get involved in the political process. He was very active in Liberal Party politics, having served himself as press secretary to the then Minister of State (Urban Affairs) and Chief Political Organizer for Quebec, the Honourable André Ouellett, and in other senior political roles within the federal Liberal government.

Living in Victoria at that time, I decided to work on the 1979 federal election campaign of David Anderson when he ran in a riding in a western community of Victoria. David lost that election, and with the Joe Clark government being defeated on a motion of non—confidence nine months later in 1980. I worked on David Anderson's unsuccessful 1980 election and following my Order—in—Council appointment as Assistant Deputy Minister in the British Columbia Ministry of Forests, I had to stay away from partisan politics. This did not stop me, however, from studying part time and completing a Master of Public Administration degree from the University of Victoria. In 1987, shortly after Bill Vander Zalm became BC's Premier, I left the provincial government and re—joined Deloitte & Touche in management consulting. At that time I also reconnected with my Liberal colleagues in Victoria and I became active again in the Saanich—Gulf Islands Federal Liberal Association. In 1990 I supported the Leadership candidacy of Jean Chrétien and it was during this leadership campaign when I met Roy MacLaren, who at the time was the MP for Etobicoke North in Toronto. I was host to a breakfast for leadership delegates and potential delegates and Roy MacLaren was my invited guest speaker. Roy was also supporting Jean Chrétien. My wife Ethne and I were seated for breakfast with Roy and his charming wife, Lee. I told them that having recently been recruited by the Noranda Forest Group, that Ethne and I would be moving to Toronto in three weeks time. Roy MacLaren told me to call him once we were settled and suggested we have lunch. Some months later I called Roy and he and I had lunch at a downtown Toronto restaurant. It was at that luncheon meeting when Roy asked if I would join the executive of his Etobicoke North federal Liberal riding association to serve as treasurer. I gladly accepted and served in that capacity until, in 1996, while he was serving as Canada's International Trade Minister, and doing a great job, he was named by Prime Minister Chrétien to serve in the prestigious role of Canada's High Commissioner (Ambassador) to Great Britain.

Roy's diplomatic posting caught all of us by surprise, but in the world of politics nothing stands still for long. Roy's departure paved the way for a by—election in Etobicoke North, together with five other by—elections across Canada. That Roy MacLaren had resigned his seat on January 24th, 1996, and the by—election was called for March 25, 1996 meant that there was no time to lose. I decided that at age fifty, I would have to run then or never – and, after some serious discussions with my wife, I decided to take the plunge. A call to Roy MacLaren, and the stalwart President of the Etobicoke North Federal Riding Association, Diarmuid Horgan, and with the Ontario Campaign Chair, Hon. David Smith (now Senator Smith) convinced me that the job was worth fighting for and that I had a good chance for success.

Thus began the treadmill which included running against, and ultimately defeating three other candidates for the Liberal nomination, and then running in the March 25th by—election campaign against six other candidates.

Sorry I missed you

During election campaigns, most of my time was spent knocking on the doors of my constituents trying to convince them, in thirty seconds or less, why they should vote for me. Actually, the primary purpose of these calls was not to enter into a huge debate on doorsteps on the pros and cons of various policies or competing platforms; but rather to introduce myself to voters and show them that I had made the effort to call upon them and make a personal appeal for their support. Since this type of canvassing occurred morning, afternoon and evening during the campaigns, in some instances no one was at home. For these constituents, a *Sorry I missed you* card was left in their mailbox or door handle which was signed by me and provided some brief information, including the coordinates of the campaign office, for those who wished to contact me. To save time signing each card during the canvass, I got into the habit of pre—signing these *Sorry I missed you* cards in advance and stockpiling them in the campaign office. Not all canvasses are done by the political candidate. Teams of canvassers work various parts of the riding, leaving campaign literature with voters as they go. Unfortunately, one group grabbed a pile of the pre—signed *Sorry I missed you* cards and began leaving them at the homes of constituents where no one answered the door. A short time later a call came into the campaign office from a voter who said that he was left a *Sorry I missed you* card that was signed by me but he had noted when he looked out of his window that I was not personally present with this group of canvassers. Obviously he had chosen not to answer his door, as is often the case, when the canvassers had knocked on his door. The gentleman argued, with good reason that it was deceptive to try and give the impression that the candidate was the one who had knocked on his door. In fact, I had been canvassing in another part of the riding at the time. I called this constituent and apologized for the mistake. I learned a good lesson from this awkward and difficult experience. From then on, any cards signed by me were kept under my control so that this would not happen again.

Election campaigns can be fun, but five of them were enough for me. By—elections, like my first campaign in 1996, can be particularly challenging, because voters often use them to send a message to the governing party. We also know from research that citizens vote almost exclusively for the political party and the party leader, with only about 10% of their voting intentions dedicated to the individual candidate. Therefore, if voters are not pleased with the party and its leader, getting elected under this banner can be difficult. Fortunately for me, in 1996, Canadians were not displeased with the performance of Jean Chrétien and the Liberal Party, but in Etobicoke North, and in the other five by—elections held in eastern Canada in 1996, there was an opportunity to displace the Bloc Québecois with the Reform Party as the Official Opposition. At that time, the Bloc held a one seat advantage over the Reform Party in the House of Commons so a swing of two seats to the Reform Party, with no growth in the Bloc seats, would give the Reformers the Official Opposition role – and all of the advantages that go along with that.

In my riding of Etobicoke North, the Reform Party campaign theme became "Boot the Bloc". This idea had some resonance for Ontarians who were not very happy having a Québec separatist party as the official opposition. With the help of many caucus colleagues, and with a lot of hard work, I was able to secure 44% of the vote – more than enough to send me to Ottawa.

For this campaign, and for the general election that swiftly followed in 1997, I was fortunate to have a very experienced campaign manager, Tom Allison, and a dedicated and hardworking team. When I asked Tom what we needed to do to win he laid out the strategy that made sense to me. When I asked him what I needed to do as the candidate to win, he narrowed it down to two essential missions – launching the fundraising team, and then knocking on doors. This I did successfully for five elections, thanks in large part to a great team of supporters and a lot of hard work. I enjoyed election campaigns at their start, but found them quite repetitive towards the end. By the end of the campaign I was always exhausted after campaigning morning, afternoon and evening, seven days a week (with the exception of Sunday mornings). During my first two campaigns I lost about fifteen pounds and wore out a pair of shoes each time.

I raised money for my election campaigns through fundraising activities by working with the Etobicoke North Federal Liberal Riding Association, my fundraising Chair, and Association Treasurer. A friend from days at Bishop's University, and for years thereafter, Mike Somerville, was my very capable riding treasurer and official agent. The official agent role came into play during election campaigns to ensure that all Elections Canada rules were being followed and that the campaign budget was being adhered to. For all five of my election campaigns, a former Noranda colleague and good friend of mine, Bill Deeks, generously and effectively acted as my fundraising chair.

Each federal riding has a limit set by Elections Canada as to how much can be spent by a candidate in each election. This amount varies by the type of riding and the geography it covers. In my typically urban riding of Etobicoke North, the election spending limit is about $75,000 per campaign. I never spent this much in any of my five federal election campaigns, and usually the amount was closer to $40,000 to $60,000 depending on the timing of the campaign and the mood of the electorate. Whenever I have mentioned these Canadian election campaign limits to U.S. Senators or Members of the U.S. House of Representatives, they shrug in disbelief, once they compare the huge amounts of money spent on elections south of the border.

Until the election financing rules were significantly changed a few years ago, I would often have a fundraising event in the riding every one—two years, depending on the state of the coffers and the expected timing of an election, at which time I could generate about $30,000 in net contributions after expenses. A reception, with a special guest like Minister of Finance Paul Martin or Deputy Prime Minister Anne McLellan, and a ticket price of $200—$250 would attract about 150 guests, often local business leaders, who would munch on hor d'oerves and sip on wine, as my special guest and myself mixed and mingled. We would of course have some speeches and a short question and answer period after the Minister's remarks. During the election campaign my riding association often hosted a lower budget event to attract individual supporters and family small business operators. Another good friend, Peter Stinson, graciously chaired these events. With the elimination of corporate donations, fundraising efforts have changed dramatically and are now focused almost exclusively on 'rank—and—file' supporters. In addition to this, money flows from Elections Canada to riding associations and the Liberal Party, under the new rules, based on the number of votes garnered in the previous election.

I was fortunate to have a good friend from university days in la belle province, John Colfer, whose company had the exclusive distribution rights for Lagostina™ cookware in Canada. Needless to say, he has done alright with that franchise which requires that all quality Lagostina™ products imported into Canada go through his company. Over many years, when corporate donations were permitted, he would ship to me, from his warehouse in Montreal to my constituency office, a substantial supply, within any applicable contribution limits, of Lagostina™ cookware sets, each valued at the retail level at between $300 and $700 each. This act of generosity and friendship proved to be extremely useful for me, and provided him with a marketing advantage as well. When asked by a local charity or agency in Etobicoke North that was organizing a fundraiser or other event for their own benefit, I would offer a set of Lagostina™ pots and pans for a raffle, silent auction, or door prize for their function. The program would credit me with making the donation and John's Lagostina™ product was always mentioned in the same breath – a win/win situation for both of us. I truly appreciated this kind gesture from my friend because without the supply of his products I would have had to decline a contribution to many worthwhile community events. Local community leaders were also thrilled with such a quality and well known product. Politically, the rub off was very positive.

Approaches to political fundraising vary by riding and by individual. Of course, with the complete banning of corporate and union donations, fundraising strategies have been irrevocably altered.

A number of my colleagues, in particular Lloyd St. Amand, Art Eggleton, Dan McTeague, Steve Mahoney and Benoit (Ben) Serré, chose an annual golf tournament as their main fundraising effort. Golf tournaments involve an incredible amount of work and for my riding of Etobicoke North I concluded that the costs of such an event, both in terms of time and money, exceeded the benefits. We had other ways to more effectively and more efficiently raise money for our election campaigns - formats that fit better in Etobicoke North. These colleagues, however, were always anxious for members of the Liberal caucus to participate in these tournaments so they could include us in the foursomes of paying participants; and so, as an act of duty and loyalty, I gladly obliged.

Ben was the MP for Temiskaming—French River from 1993 to 1997 followed byTemiskaming— Cochrane from 1997 to 2004 when the riding boundaries were re—drawn. This riding in Northern Ontario was a long drive, but Ben and his supporters were always very appreciative when colleagues from southern Ontario made the effort to join him and his team for his golf tournament.

Lloyd St. Amand, MP for Brant (Brantford), is another colleague whose annual golf tournament I attended regularly. For both tournaments that were hosted by Ben and Lloyd, I would donate a prize, usually a set of Lagostina™ cookware or an autographed copy of my book, The Poverty of Corrupt Nations.

In some rural ridings, a $200 reception is not feasible, so often fundraisers there take the form of sit down dinners for $30—$50, or a reception priced at $20—$30. With skinny profit margins on events like this, it is necessary to replicate them many times over if one wishes to raise the money needed to run a campaign.

The other key component for a successful election campaign is a strong group of volunteers. These are the people who do door—to—door canvassing; make telephone calls to elicit support; put up election signs throughout the riding; assist with the development and publishing of brochures; organize community meetings and prepare for all—candidates meetings; liaise with the media and set up interviews, and perform many other critical functions. These volunteers come from every walk of life and are motivated to help for different reasons. Some are committed ideologically to the political party they support and assist in the election campaign to help their candidate win. Others, for a variety of reasons, are unhappy with the party in power or the official opposition party and are working for change. There are volunteers who show up because they anticipate they may need the help of their elected MP in the future so they bet on one candidate and work to keep him/her in office or elected. The goal of working in an MP's office inspires some people to work hard on the campaign to leave open the possibility for future employment. Others get involved simply for the fun of it and as an opportunity to socialize and network. Political 'junkies' also play an energetic role.

For my election campaigns we typically worked with up to 200—300 volunteers by the end of the campaign. The number of volunteers grew as the election campaign progressed, and the core group of volunteers – the ones who did most of the work – was a smaller group of 70—80.

Election campaigning is divided into two distinct phases –
1. identifying who your supporters are; and
2. getting your supporters to vote on election day.

During the canvassing phase, supporters are identified through a number of mechanisms –
- door—to door canvassing;
- telephone canvassing;
- data bases developed from previous elections;
- voters contacting the campaign office offering their support; and
- other means.

Data is entered every day to identify supporters. On election day, or e—day, calls are made, and visits are made, to these supporters encouraging them to go to the polls to vote, and where needed, transportation to and from the polling station and any other help needed to assist in this process.

Because of the diverse make—up of my riding, leading up to each election and during the election campaign I drew on the advice of a Community Outreach Advisory Committee which met periodically with me. The composition of the committee consisted of community leaders and my supporters in the Sikh, Hindu, Muslim, Somali, Ghanaian, Nigerian, Italian communities and other groups as well. We would have an agenda for each meeting at which time we would discuss platform and policy issues that were unique for them and their colleagues, and we would develop strategies for connecting with the various community groups by attending events, sending out targeted flyers, and a range of other options.

During election campaigns I virtually lived in the Sikh Gurdwara, the Swaminarayan Hindu Temple, the International Muslim Organization Mosque, and the various churches in the area. All-candidates meetings are also a feature of election campaigns. Regrettably I found these to be of limited value since most people who attend them have already made up their minds and are there either to try to embarrass you, or make you look good.

Some amusing things can happen on the election trail, even if at the time the humour might escape you. Three such incidents come to mind.

In the hard—fought 1996 by—election, a writ ordering the holding of a by—election was issued on February 7, 1996. Polling day was set for Monday, March 25, 1996, or forty—seven days after the by—

election was called. This was a long election campaign, fought in the middle of a cold winter in Toronto. It was so cold we were unable to erect lawn signs in the normal way because lawns were frozen solid. My face was wind and sun—burned because I was canvassing each and every day and achieving good coverage of the riding. Of course, it is not possible to reach each and every door in the riding – even over forty—seven days.

During one canvass in an afternoon and towards the end of the campaign, I knocked on a door and was met by a gentleman who immediately uttered the following,

"Glad you finally made it here" he said. "I have been waiting for you to come to my house since early February."

Taking the high road, I retorted "Well thank you. It is not possible to knock on every door in the riding but here I am and glad that we will have the opportunity to meet and chat briefly".

The gentleman at the door began a short speech on issues he was concerned about and I listened intently. Suddenly, in the middle of a sentence, and looking at my sunburned face, he abruptly stopped what he was saying.

"I know why you haven't been around – you've been down south to the sun", he accused.

Presumably my peeling facial skin led him to this staggering conclusion. Initially I was very offended and angry. If he only knew the hours I had been logging in the bitter cold. I corrected him and it was only later that one of my supporters told me I should have said – "Yes I was down South – south of Dixon Road!" But alas I was too tired and bereft of energy at that point to engage in such humorous repartee.

I would learn later that thirty seconds maximum per door was Sheila Copp's approach. I canvassed with her in Hamilton East in the May/June by—election after she had resigned her seat over the GST issue. While I didn't adopt this approach, I understood where she was coming from. In her view, if they supported you, you should move on to the next resident; and, if they didn't support you, you weren't going to convince them otherwise at their door during an election campaign.

Another time, during the 2000 election campaign, I was canvassing in a high rise apartment building in Etobicoke North. My knock on a door led to a gentleman rushing out and hugging me and twirling around with me in the hallway. While doing this, he was vividly exhorting my virtues and describing his great affection for the Liberal Party of Canada. His son, who appeared to be about ten or twelve years of age, was standing next to the two swirling dancers, interjected at one point with the following.

"Daddy, is it possible to support more than one political party in an election campaign? " he asked.

Turning to the father, I could see that he was turning beet red. I can only imagine what he had to say to his son after we had left!

Another unusual event occurred during the 1997 election campaign, I walked down a cul—de—sac and knocked on the door of a home directly across from a school yard. The husband and wife complained bitterly that young people were jumping the school fence at night and making a big disturbance with music, other noise, and perhaps using alcohol and/or drugs. I asked them if they had reported these events to the local police. They said they had done so on many occasions – with little or no affect. I told them I would speak to the city councillor for their ward and see if there was something that could be done. They thanked me and I continued with the canvass. Later that evening at the campaign office, I discovered that the relevant city councillor, Mario Giansante, was in my campaign office making telephone calls on my behalf. It was no secret in the community that Mario was a big Liberal Party supporter. I gave Mario the information and he called our mutual constituents right then on the spot. He told them he would ask the City of Toronto Division 23 police officers to send more patrols into their area – a promise he kept. Were these parents ever impressed! Mario told me that, based on such a same day turnaround, they would be voting for me, and also voting for Mario in the next municipal election!

Some disturbing things can happen during election campaigns – like handing out hundreds of brochures to canvassers only to find out later that the brochures had been ditched and the canvassers retired to a local pub. It means starting over again and it amounts to a huge betrayal.

Every election campaign is fraught with cases of vandalized signs and/or stolen campaign signs and it is usually impossible to establish who the culprits are.

On one trip to a high rise complex, some distance away from the campaign office and with a canvassing crew of some ten—twelve individuals, we were denied entry into this gated community.

"No canvassers allowed" we were told, even though our supporters in some of the buildings had told us the Reform Party had been inside distributing campaign pamphlets.

I reminded the security guard at the gate that the under the *Canada Elections Act* it is illegal to deny candidates or their representatives access to an apartment or condominium building from 9:00 a.m. to 9:00 p.m. for the purpose of canvassing door—to—door. At that point he told me that he would call his supervisor for clarification which he did and told us that he was not able to get through to his boss. I told him that unless he let us onto the property within five minutes, I would have no choice but to call the police. Five minutes came and went. I called the police and told the guard what I had done. Magically and mysteriously, he then advised me that he had made contact with his supervisor and he had received permission to lift the barrier and let us through. As we passed his booth I said thank you to the security guard and commented.

"I guess I lost your vote" I said.

"Not necessarily" was his reply.

Reading between the lines, I came to the conclusion that his supervisor, perhaps a Reform Party supporter, had consciously decided not to let me into the complex to canvass, and the guard at the gate respected the fact that I wouldn't put up with that type of foul play.

So this is how the electoral process in Canada works. Win the nomination to represent your party of choice, and then fight like a dog to win the election. Sir Winston Churchill once said "It has been said that democracy is the worst form of government except (*for*) all the others that have been tried"[34].

It was reassuring to me, in the way that people reacted in 2009 to Prime Minister Harper's decision to prorogue parliament for the second time in two years, that Canadians really care about their parliament. Cynics would argue that the reason for the outcry from citizens is because they like to see their MPs working, and not 'sloughing off' during a two month prorogation. For some, this is causing the angst, but I believe the majority of Canadians are angry because parliament has been denied the important role it has been granted – to hold the government to account, to pass laws and to make decisions in the best interest of all Canadians.

When I am traveling abroad I take great pride when I am asked at a border crossing why I have a 'Special' Canadian Passport, and what a Member of the Queen's Privy Council for Canada is. I still get goose bumps when I reply that I was a representative in Canada's House of Commons for a number of years. When I walk along Wellington Street in Ottawa today

---

34   www.quotationspage.com

and gaze at the Parliament Buildings, the Centre Block, the Peace Tower, those goose bumps of respect and awe for the institution of parliament, that I first experienced in 1996 as a rookie MP, return to me.

We must retain that pride in our national parliamentary institutions. We must re—engage Canadians in our political processes. We have to keep the goose bumps alive.

APPENDIX 1 :
Question Period and Follow—up
Adjournment Proceeding (Late Show)

-Question Period June 8th, 2006

"Hon. Roy Cullen (Etobicoke North, Lib.):

Mr. Speaker, yesterday the Minister of Natural Resources claimed that the wind power production incentive was not cut from the budget. But what he was careful not to mention was that the credits not yet allocated have been frozen, which actually paralyzes the program and any action in this sector.

Why has the minister decided to create such uncertainty for this sector and to hang wind energy technology out to dry?

Hon. Gary Lunn (Minister of Natural Resources, CPC):

Mr. Speaker, we are developing our plan. At committee earlier this morning, I asked the hon. member to bring forward his ideas.

I applaud the NDP members. I was quite surprised that after I asked them to submit their ideas and indicated that we were interested in talking to them, only a few hours later they actually came up with some suggestions.

We are moving forward with proposals that will have a meaningful impact on every single Canadian. We believe wind will play a future role in Canada's energy supply and we support that.

Hon. Roy Cullen (Etobicoke North, Lib.):

Mr. Speaker, we know what works. It was in our programs, but there is more.

The government pretends it wants to meet an ethanol target of 5%. However, we now learn that the government has let the ethanol expansion program die. There is no new funding for wind energy, no new funding for biofuels, and the government is cutting the EnerGuide home program.

Is this the government's only response to global warming, scrapping and freezing programs without one single new idea of its own, not one?

Hon. Gary Lunn (Minister of Natural Resources, CPC):

Mr. Speaker, if the member opposite wants to talk about the programs that were working for the Liberal Party, I do not know if he is talking about the sponsorship program or what he is referring to, the facts speak for themselves.

Greenhouse gases under the old Liberal government, the very old Liberal government, went up each and every single year it was in office for 13 years. We have done more in six months than that old government did in 13 years.

I want to remind the hon. member, on renewable fuels, that the Minister of Agriculture and Agri—Food, the Minister of the Environment, and I met with every provincial counterpart, and we are moving forward to bringing real results to every single Canadian".[35]

---

35   Canada House of Commons Hansard—36 (June 8th, 2006) Line 1430

1. Adjournment Proceedings September 27, 2006

"A motion to adjourn the House under Standing Order 38 deemed to have been moved.

* * *

Natural Resources

Hon. Roy Cullen (Etobicoke North, Lib.):

Mr. Speaker, I was listening to the member for Red Deer talk about the importance of wind energy at a time when the government has cancelled or frozen the program.

The Canadian wind energy sector is emerging as one of the key components in our energy mix for the next 20 years. As traditional sources of fuels and energies peak and dwindle, wind energy will remain strong and viable as there is nearly a limitless supply. The Liberal Party and the Liberal government recognized this. That is why in budget 2005 we committed to an expanded wind energy incentive by quadrupling the previous program and committing $200 million over five years.

Unfortunately, it would seem that this is not as clear to the Conservatives as it is to us. Perhaps some data will help them understand better.

The Canadian wind energy industry has shown impressive growth with an average annual increase of over 30% for the last five years. A recent report shows that wind energy firms are optimistic about future growth.

Globally, wind energy capacity increased from 18,000 megawatts to 59,000 megawatts between 2000 and 2005, and now produces enough power to meet the needs of more than 17 million homes. By 2010, global installed wind energy capacity is expected to be 149,000 megawatts.

As an example, wind energy met 20% of electricity demand in Denmark, 8% in Spain, 5% in Germany and 4% in Portugal and Ireland. Wind energy could easily meet 15% to 20% of Canada's total electricity needs based on an initial target of 10,000 megawatts by 2010, which would take us to about 4% of Canada's total electricity needs. Experience in other countries is clearly demonstrating that wind energy can make substantive and significant contributions to total electricity supplied.

Further, the wind energy industry can create jobs. Every one megawatt of installed wind energy capacity in Canada generates $1.5 million in investment and creates 2.5 direct and 8 indirect person years of employment. If 5% of Canada's electricity was generated by wind energy in 2015, such development would produce $19.5 billion in investment and create 32,500 direct and 104,000 indirect person years of employment.

In the last session, the Minister of Natural Resources claimed that the Conservative government did not scrap funding for the wind power production incentive program, but what he later admitted was that funding had been frozen, effectively paralyzing the program and creating uncertainty for this industry.

In a May 26 letter from Mr. Robert Hornung, the president of the Canadian Wind Energy Association, to the Minister of Natural Resources, Mr. Hornung made it clear that the freezing of funds within the wind power production incentive program has had a serious negative effect on the industry. He said:

The fact that WPPI [wind power production incentive program] funds are frozen has made it difficult for the Federal Government to continue to work with projects currently in the process to obtain funds under the WPPI program. For example, projects must work with the Federal Government on a federal environmental assessment in order to have access to WPPI [the wind power production incentive program]. These processes have slowed down significantly or halted. As a result, valuable time is being lost for projects who are working to be in a position to access WPPI if the expansion proceeds. This means delay in ultimately getting these projects into the ground where they can provide significant economic benefits to local communities across Canada.

This is proof that the Conservative government cutbacks are hurting the industry and costing jobs for Canadians. As we have seen with the scrapping of the popular one tonne challenge and other programs, these are ideologically driven. I would ask the government to reinstate this very important program.

Mr. Christian Paradis (Parliamentary Secretary to the Minister of Natural Resources, CPC):

Mr. Speaker, I am pleased to respond today to the question asked by my hon. colleague, the member for Etobicoke North. The hon. member is concerned about the alleged cuts to programs. We know that programs such as EnerGuide or the one tonne challenge were deemed ineffective.

That is why the current government is now looking into more effective programs.

I would like to remind the hon. member that the Minister of Finance made a $2 billion commitment to the environment and energy efficiency in the budget he brought down.

This is a significant investment. We think such an investment can be better used and provide better results than the money spent by the previous government.

Our government promised to pursue new directions in matters of climate change policy. We want a plan to reduce greenhouse gas emissions, a plan that takes into account the economic, social and environmental context of our country. We want to establish a plan that ensures clean air, water, soil and energy for Canadians—an effective and realistic way for Canada to address issues related to climate change.

It is not enough to do what the previous government did, which was to make an international commitment without developing a plan to honour that commitment and without determining what impact it might have on Canada. We have seen the results of that approach. Years after the Liberal government adopted programs and spent hundreds of millions of dollars on climate change initiatives, we are still far from achieving significant results and very far from meeting our commitments. The Liberals set a target of reducing greenhouse gas emissions by 6%. Today, Canada's emissions are 35% above that target.

It is time to restructure our programs, and that is what we are doing. We have to find the best way of using this money for maximum impact on climate change.

Some of the current programs can be tailored to our strategy. In other cases, however, we will have to decide whether taxpayers' money might not be better used to support the new strategy. All the climate change initiatives are being reviewed, to make sure they produce real results for Canada.

My friend mentioned the EnerGuide program and the one tonne challenge. On re—evaluating these initiatives, the government concluded that taxpayers' money could be better used and spent on initiatives that will be more effective in reducing greenhouse gas emissions.

The government is developing a new strategy to reduce greenhouse gas emissions. As my friend is aware, the various ministers with responsibility in this area will be announcing specific initiatives in the coming weeks.

The House will then see the wisdom of investing in programs that will have a real impact on air, water, soil and energy quality for Canadians.

Hon. Roy Cullen:

Mr. Speaker, while the government hides behind reviews, studies and platitudes, Canadian workers and the industry are suffering.

We have heard a lot about this Conservative government's "made in Canada" approach to our greenhouse gas and climate change problems, but to date the government has not given us anything concrete, only promises and hot air.

While the Prime Minister talks of Canada's energy resources to his friends in the Republican Party, his government is squandering and choking off a burgeoning energy industry by refusing to commit to the renewal and expansion of the wind power production incentive.

Does the parliamentary secretary have the courage to look up from his prepared text and commit to the House tonight that his backward and hypocritical government will do the right thing for a change and unfreeze and expand the wind power production incentive?

Mr. Christian Paradis:

Mr. Speaker, let us be clear. We arrived here in power as a new government and emissions are 35% over the previous government's target, and we are being asked to manage responsibly. In the meantime, while we are waiting for a new made in Canada solution to be implemented, the government is managing some 95 different programs that address climate change. These programs will continue in the current fiscal year and temporary financial assistance will be available, as is already the case. As I was saying earlier, the ministers concerned will make relevant announcements on specific programs.

From the beginning we realized that some programs were not achieving the desired results. My colleague referred to the One Tonne Challenge, for example, a marketing campaign run by the previous government. We do not want to adopt that approach. We want to use taxpayers' money in a way that will achieve the best results. We want to implement more effective and efficient programs to reduce emissions in a responsible manner.

We will continue to review current activities and support those that work. Furthermore, we are planning to add new activities that will help improve performance for all Canadians. We are committed to establishing a strategy that will ensure the quality of air, water, soil and energy.

The Acting Speaker (Mr. Andrew Scheer):

The motion to adjourn the House is now deemed to have been adopted. The House stands adjourned until tomorrow at 10 a.m. pursuant to Standing Order 24(1).

(The House adjourned at 7:18 p.m.)"[36]

---

[36] Canada House of Commons Hansard (English versions only)—(September 27th, 2006)

About the Author

Born in 1944 in Montreal, Canada, Roy Cullen earned his B.A. in Business Administration, and a Master of Public Administration. He qualified as a Canadian Chartered Accountant in 1972. Initially elected to the House of Commons in Ottawa in a by-election in 1996, he was re-elected in the 1997, 2000, 2004, and the 2006 general elections. He retired from the Canadian House of Commons in 2008. During his career prior to 1996, Mr. Cullen served as an assistant deputy minister in the British Columbia Ministry of Forests, and as a vice-president in the Noranda Forest Group (now Norbord).

As a member of the Prime Minister Jean Chrétien's government, and later under Prime Minister Paul Martin, Mr. Cullen served as chair of the House of Commons Standing Committee on Finance, as parliamentary secretary to the minister of finance, as parliamentary secretary to the deputy prime minister and the minister for public safety and emergency preparedness; and as chair of the Ontario Liberal caucus. In 2006 he was sworn-in as a member of the Queen's Privy Council for Canada. He also served as Official Opposition critic for natural resources.

In March 2004, Mr. Cullen orchestrated the passage of a complex private members' *Bill C-212, An act respecting user fees*, by engaging members of parliament and senators. The Bill was passed and resulted in significant changes to government user fees, making the system more transparent, performance-based, and accountable.

During his tenure as parliamentary secretary to the minister of finance, Mr. Cullen was actively involved in designing and implementing Canada's anti-money-laundering regime. Mr. Cullen has been very active with the Global Organization of Parliamentarians Against Corruption (GOPAC) in the international fight against corruption and money laundering.

Mr. Cullen lives in Victoria, B.C., Canada, with his wife, Ethne. They have one son, Peter.

www.ingramcontent.com/pod-product-compliance
Lightning Source LLC
Chambersburg PA
CBHW021602280526
45784CB00001BA/470